CLEMATIS
for all Seasons

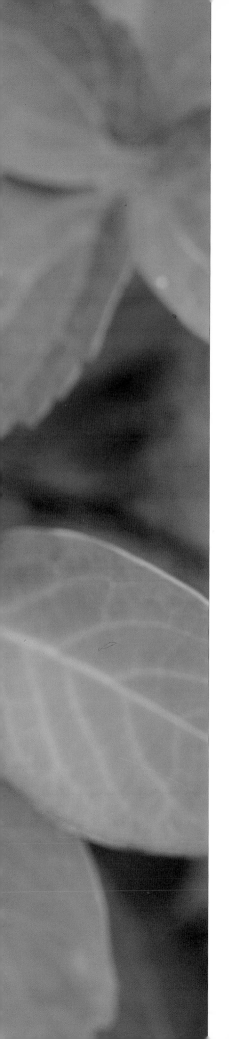

CLEMATIS
for all Seasons

John Feltwell

FIREFLY BOOKS

A FIREFLY BOOK

Clematis for all Seasons
Published by Firefly Books 1999

Cataloguing in Publication Data

Feltwell, John
Clematis for all seasons

Includes index.
ISBN 1-55209-283-6
1. Clematis. I. Title.
SB413.C6F44 1999   635.9'3334   C98–932462–1

Published in the United States in 1999 by Firefly Books (U.S.) Inc.
P.O. Box 1338, Ellicott Station, Buffalo, New York 14205

Published in Canada in 1999 by Firefly Books Ltd.
3680 Victoria Park Avenue, Willowdale, Ontario, Canada M2H 3K1

A Berry Book, conceived, edited and designed by Susan Berry
for Collins & Brown Limited.
First published in Great Britain in 1999 by Collins & Brown Limited,
London House, Great Eastern Wharf, Parkgate Road, London SW11 4NQ.

Editor Amanda Lebentz
Art director Roger Bristow
Designer Helen Collins
Cover design David Fordham

Printed in Hong Kong.

CONTENTS

Foreword

By Mary Toomey M.Sc., Ph.D.
Editor, *The Clematis*,
journal of the British Clematis Society

"AGE CANNOT WITHER HER, nor custom stale her infinite variety." These Shakespearean words may very well describe the magical, most charming and rewarding genus, *Clematis*. Often referred to as the queen of vines, the genus that belongs to the buttercup family also encompasses a number of garden-worthy herbaceous plants. How very fortunate we gardeners are to be able to choose and grow an enormous variety and number of clematis—species and cultivars—almost year-round.

Enjoying an unprecedented popularity as a garden plant admirably suited for growing on its own, in association with trees, shrubs, roses and other vines, among hardy perennials and even as ground cover, clematis can rightly be called a plant for all seasons, people and places. This very versatile plant can even be grown in containers, given routine care and provided that the right variety—and there are plenty of them—is chosen. The decade of the 1990s belongs to the clematis and an ever-increasing number of new cultivars from Japan, Sweden, Holland, New Zealand, Poland, Estonia, Russia and the U.K. are being added to the already long list in the Royal Horticultural Society's *The RHS Plant Finder*, which is revised each year.

This is only to be expected because there is an astonishing myriad of flower colors and forms—ranging from the reds, purples and blues of the large-flowered cultivars to the cascades of small, starry, white blooms of sweet, autumn clematis. There may not yet be a truly large, yellow-flowered cultivar to delight gardeners, but there are plenty to choose from the oriental species and their hybrids, which boast waxy, yellow flowers. There is a clematis to fit every gardener's needs and pleasures and, equally important, there is a great need for an authoritative source of sound knowledge and advice on how to select and cultivate this charming plant.

This is where the author John Feltwell very cleverly brings together in one volume all the knowledge required by gardeners to help them choose and grow clematis by dealing with the subject under much-needed and long-awaited headings such as "Clematis by Group and Season" and "Clematis by Color". This novel treatment of the genus is greatly enhanced by a wealth of splendid photographs. At a glance, any gardener should be able to decide on a clematis by color and incorporate it into an existing color scheme in the garden or create a new dream garden full of clematis. In *Clematis for all Seasons*, there are many examples of clematis to suit every garden—small or big, any location, aspect and every season.

This undoubtedly very popular garden plant has unfortunately been associated for far too long with unnecessary myths, which have discouraged many novice gardeners from growing clematis with confidence. The refreshing, no-nonsense approach adopted by the author to all aspects of choosing, planting, pruning, caring for and maintaining clematis should banish much of the mystique surrounding these plants.

I have no doubt that this is a book that gardeners with a passion for clematis will visit and revisit frequently.

Clematis in their habitat

*Clematis, like roses, are typical Northern hemisphere plants,
restricted in their natural state to temperate regions from Western Europe
and Asia to North America.*

WITH OVER 200 native species of clematis known around the world, there is much to choose from and many suitable to grow in the garden. Most of the native species have Latin names, although a few have common English names.

There is a lot of useful information tied up in common names. If you know from which kind of habitat the species clematis comes (mountains, woodland, marsh etc), then you have a good idea of the regime it is used to. Those species originating from the hot, dry Mediterranean climate might naturally be better prepared for drought conditions under a hot sun. There are certain characteristics of clematis growing wild in their own habitat that are particularly appealing and that have been passed on

C. alpina A.G.M.
LEFT *With more foliage than flowers, this is how the wild alpina clematis grows in the European Alps, sending filigrees of shoots through roadside shrubs and trees.*

C. flammula
ABOVE *This Mediterranean native was first introduced to England in 1560. From mid-summer onward, it produces hundreds of almond-scented, star-like flowers.*

C. maximowicziana
ABOVE *Sprawling through vegetation in shady North American woods where it is native, this vigorous plant and prolific flowerer is also known as* C. terniflora.

C. vitalba
LEFT *Known as old man's beard, this vigorous vine grows best in alkaline soils and is native to Europe. It has scented flowers and fluffy seeds.*

to many clematis grown in gardens. One of these is vigor, the other is hardiness.

To see *C. alpina* A.G.M. shining through wayside vegetation or small conifers high in the European Alps is to admire its dogged persistence and hardiness in extremes of climate at a height of 8,700ft. (2,900m.). Or, to see the foaming coat of white and cream flowers of *C. maximowicziana* in a Maine woodland is to admire its wildness, its effervescence and its dominance over all other vegetation in the autumn.

This clematis out-performs all other autumn flowers in its native eastern U.S.A., which is typical of clematis species since they always do best in their natural habitats in the wild. Transplant them to the comforts of an herbaceous border against the warmth of a brick wall, and they may also perform well for you.

Grow *C. vitalba* or *C. flammula* in the garden, and gardening will be a matter of control not nurture. *C. vitalba* has a habit of swamping yew woods in southeast England and overflowing the woodland canopy at 40ft. (13m.) with its liana-like swags of growth. *C. apiifolia* grows well against a wall and gives a similar showing to *C. vitalba* and *C. flammula*. Among the many bell-shaped native species are the purple bells of *C. crispa* and the tulip-like, red and yellow colors of *C. texensis*.

C. armandii
ABOVE *Reliable as they come, the scented armandii clematis are natives of China and powerful growers. They also have evergreen foliage.*

C. microphylla
LEFT *The delicate and tiny sepals of this Australian evergreen vine are like propellers. A species of hot sunny habitats, its place in the garden has to be chosen with care.*

C. viorna
LEFT *The reflexed bells of this native northeastern American plant give an unusual splash of color to shrubs through which it will grow. It is named the leather flower, after its leathery feel, as well as the vase vine, after the shape of its flowers.*

C. koreana
LEFT *A native of Korea, C. koreana has fragrant, bell-shaped flowers, which may be creamy yellow, red or dull violet in color.*

C. texensis
LEFT *Originally from the southern U.S. state of Texas, the brightly colored C. texensis is much used in the hybridisation of clematis.*

Breeding

With some 700 different names of clematis commonly listed, about one-tenth of which are synonyms, the world of clematis would appear to be a confusing place. In fact there are about 120 basic types of clematis from which all the rest have arisen as hybrids and clones.

THE SPECIES clematis are the mainstay of the genetic diversity within the genus and it is not surprising that some clematis enthusiasts only grow species clematis. They come with natural hardiness and resistance, which are always welcome virtues. The few antipodean clematis are a side group within the species clematis and are mostly alpines. The other groups of clematis are all named after their origins, thus the alpinas are related to *C. alpina* A.G.M., the montanas (all 60 named ones) all related to *C. montana* and so on.

It may be that there is debate over the origins of some, whether they are more related to alpinas or macropetalas, but this is for those who study plant taxonomy. Once you have seen and understood the characteristics of the species clematis, then you are a long way toward understanding and identifying the group that a clematis belongs to. Thus, the beautiful bells of *C. texensis* are reflected in *C.t.* 'Gravetye Beauty' or *C.t.* 'Etoile Rose'. In some hybrids, the origin of the plant is shown by an appropriate letter after the name, thus *C.* 'Elvan' (Vt) means that it belongs to the viticella group.

Natural variation

In the chapter, Clematis by Group and Season, different types of clematis have been looked at according to their botanical origins and in seasonal order starting, for instance, with the alpinas and macropetalas, which welcome in the early spring, and moving on to montanas, viticellas, integrifolias, the texensis group, heracleifolias, tanguticas and the orientalis group.

Selection of hybrids of clematis has been aided by the natural phenomenon of variation, which is nature's way of throwing up all sorts of different forms in a natural population of plants. When a

Crossed hybrids

This shows what crossing of hybrids can do. Here, two dissimilar parents have produced a new clematis "gem"—but the hybridisation has not given the offspring increased vigor since it shares its parents' lack of oomph!

C. 'Lincoln Star'

C. 'Mrs N. Thompson'

C. 'Scartho Gem'

10

clematis grower sees a departure from the norm, for instance a different shape, color or form, he or she can then propagate that plant by making cuttings, thus ensuring that subsequent plants will breed true. By repeatedly selecting for a particular characteristic, a new hybrid or cultivar can be produced and subsequently named. Another way of producing hybrids is to make the crosses between two different types in the hope that some of the characteristics of each parent are combined. Here, some skill is required, since the pollen from the anthers of one plant is rubbed on to the ripe stigmas of the other. The plants have to be grown in controlled conditions (see page 104) to stop pollinating insects transfering pollen, until fertilisation has been accomplished. In nature, variation among clematis carries on repeatedly, improving the stock. In some cases, clematis enthusiasts see a clone of a clematis which is different from others known and propagate vegetatively from this, thus introducing more variety into the trade. The range and scope of artificial crossings is infinite, as more and more hybrids are brought on to the market each year. A species crossed with a hybrid can also produce good results, as indeed the cross made by the Jackmans (of jackmanii fame) in 1890 when they produced *C. texensis* 'Sir Trevor Lawrence' from a cross between *C. texensis* (the true species) and *C.* 'Star of India' A.G.M.

C. 'Comtesse de Bouchaud A.G.M.

Shared traits
'John Huxtable' was a chance seedling from 'Comtesse de Bouchaud' A.G.M. and has retained many of its parent's characteristics, except the flowers are creamy white in color.

C. 'John Huxtable'

Family characteristics
When the Jackmans crossed C. texensis with C. 'Star of India' in 1890 they produced the similar-colored C. texensis 'Sir Trevor Lawrence'.

C. texensis

C. 'Star of India'

C. texensis 'Sir Trevor Lawrence'

What clematis where?

*Clematis is one of the most versatile groups of plants
and examples can be found for almost all parts of the garden,
whether on a warm or cold wall.*

CLEMATIS ARE best shown off against a wall or growing up a tree trunk or old stump. Most are climbers and various types can be selected for full sun, dappled light or full shade. For evergreen foliage try any of the scented *C. armandii* hybrids. Then there are the herbaceous types, which are perennials that die down over winter, and these can be used to give bulk to herbaceous borders, to flop over paths or to grow through other perennials as the year develops.

Many clematis are vigorous, but there are some dwarf forms of *C. orientalis,* for instance, that can be usefully employed in hanging baskets. And the alpine clematis from New Zealand are often well set off in containers. The vigor of clematis means that they are great performers over trellis, pergolas or arbors. The great joy of gardening with clematis is that the vast majority can be grown through, up or entangled with a fellow garden plant. The reward for all this apparently wayward growth is a riot of fat buds that emerge from an unlikely alliance to show a spectacular display of flowers. The wild nature of clematis often wins through.

There are also plenty of cultivars that are not vigorous and that, however cajoled, never produce more growth or flowers than previous years. There are even those that won't produce any flowers at all in some years. For the pleasure of seeing some clematis with a superabundance of flowers, there are always a few that never go anywhere. Hybridisation has perhaps left the vigor gene well behind. Clematis do well with roses, and many of the new hybrids are the right height and have the correct temperament to grow inside a rose bush or pillar and to merge successfully after a few months (see pages 90-91).

C. 'Hagley Hybrid'
LEFT *A reliable clematis,* C. *'Hagley Hybrid' is a good performer and produces a shower of pink flowers.*

C. recta and gladioli
ABOVE *A good subject for the herbaceous border,* C. recta *is a native of southern Europe with a profusion of fragrant flowers and is ideal in combinations.*

C. heracleifolia hybrid
LEFT *This is a clump-forming herbaceous clematis represented by a number of forms in gardens.*

C. armandii 'Apple Blossom'
RIGHT *This peach of a clematis has the rose tints of apple blossom and the double appeal of scent and subtle coloration.*

Clematis flower forms

*Although clematis flowers can be categorised into three main groups, the
variety of forms available is so enormous that when it comes to shape, size and color,
there would appear to be no common ground.*

ABOUT THE only description that applies to all clematis flowers is that they are either single, semi-double or double. Beyond that their characteristics are designed to frustrate. They can produce singles as a first showing, then doubles later. The first flowers may differ in shape from the second crop of flowers. The flowers can change in shape as they mature on the stem. The color of flowers changes as they age, and with exposure to light. A young plant can produce smaller flowers than a mature one. A pot-bound clematis can produce flowers one-third smaller than usual.

The only constant feature of clematis is that they demonstrate variation in a big way. Natural selection plays crafty tricks. The form of a clematis flower can differ completely from garden to garden,

some prime examples being 'Jackmanii Rubra', 'Barbara Dibley' or 'Nikolai Rubstov' (see pages 16–17). As a single flower unfurls, it sometimes goes through an interesting range of shapes, as in 'Lincoln Star' or 'Blue Ravine'.

Diverse characteristics

The most staggering difference is still seen between specimens of the same hybrid, such as *C.* 'Venosa Violacea'. Because of the isolation of breeding material in central and western Europe, selection has gone its own way, resulting perhaps in the extraordinarily diverse characteristics of a very attractive clematis. The Polish form of 'Venosa Violacea' has very pronounced, light and dark areas compared to the form that is photographed in England.

Types of single

There is a classification of single flowers that is very descriptive: saucer, star, open bell, bell, tulip and tubular. Single flowers are typified by having a clear number of sepals set around the central "boss", where the male and female reproductive parts (stamens and stigma) are situated. The individual sepals may have smooth or wavy edges or a central color bar running along the sepals. The tip of the sepals may be reflexed or the necessary identification features may be on the underside of the sepal.

C. 'Schneeglanz' (star)

C. texensis (bell)

C. 'Princess of Wales' (tubular)

C. crispa hybrid (tulip)

C. x *eriostemon* 'Blue Boy' (open bell)

14

Semi-double flowers

Semi-double flowers are mid-way between singles and doubles, as their name suggests. They are identified by the presence of smaller, often disfigured sepals arising from the central boss area. These extra sepals can grow to become larger sepals. The increase in number of sepals helps to give the flower a somewhat fuller image, but not as much as that from a double flower. The exuberant growth of 'Marie Boisselot' A.G.M. can produce semi-doubles, which differ significantly from the well-open and older, single flowers.

C. 'Kathleen Dunsford'

Double flowers

Double flowers are classified as either "Double, small-flowered" or "Double, large-flowered". There are few small ones but many large-flowered doubles. Double flowers have a mass of smaller sepals often surrounding and smothering the central boss area. They tend to be large and particularly attractive. It is always a source of fascination to watch a double flower form into its magnificent self. First, there is often a spidery mass of undeveloped leaves around an undeveloped flower bud. This then expands into a frequently light-colored, small boss of unopened sepals, before it bursts into its multitude of sepals, as in 'Countess of Lovelace'.

C. 'Countess of Lovelace'

C. montana 'Marjorie'

COLOR AND FORM

Color and form in clematis is likely to deceive the novice and even the seasoned
clematis expert. This is because when clematis open, they sometimes change shape and color,
and may look like completely different cultivars. Here are some examples
showing just how dramatically flowers can change within a few days as they open, or how
different they can look at various times of the year.

C. 'Duchess of Edinburgh'

*Double flowers start out with a pale, soft-centered part,
which opens out to form the full flower.*

C. 'Vyvyan Pennell' A.G.M.

*Plump with expectation, the central, white button of the
flower makes an attractive focal point. It opens out to
reveal the glamour of the whole flower.*

C. 'Marie Boisselot' A.G.M.

*Two equally attractive but distinctly different flower
shapes demonstrate the magnificence of this cultivar. The
flower on the right is fully open and the flower on the far
right is half-open.*

C. 'Blue Ravine'

*As if it were another cultivar altogether, the spiky, early
stage of the developing flower is very different to the soft,
rounded shape it will become.*

C. 'Belle of Woking'

Beautiful, double flowers are always produced, but they fade and tend to vary in their structure.

C. 'Barbara Dibley'

Looking like entirely different flowers, the variation of the sepals is very apparent here, with one plant having very narrow necks to the base of the sepals; this is probably the result of a poor seedling stock.

C. 'Nikolai Rubstov'

The long sepals in some specimens, such as that on the left, are almost spatula-shaped, whereas a more usual clematis shape is seen in others.

C. 'Venosa Violacea' A.G.M.

This flower may have more or less pronounced, central, light areas on its crisp, violet sepals, depending on the clones from which it comes. The specimen on the right is a false clone, or has not been purely bred, and is so different from the normal form that it could be given a new name.

Unusual clematis

Space restrictions or the effects of wind can often cause clematis to look atypical, stunted or disfigured, yet there are several bizarre-looking clematis that have been selected to look this way.

CLEMATIS FLOWERS get themselves into all sorts of twists and turns that do not always conform to the norm. For all its virtues *C.* 'Alba Luxurians' A.G.M., with its green-splashed sepals, looks as though something has gone radically wrong with its color palette. Attractive but easily missed as single flowers, *en masse* it can make a veritable display, especially if blanketing the top of a wall.

C. 'Wilhelmina Tull' has to be one of the wackiest clematis available, with its sepals of different lengths. The most deceitful clematis is 'Pennell's Purity', which looks so much like a camellia or double rose that it is difficult to concede it is a clematis at all.

The star-like appearance is common among all sorts of clematis, such as 'Lincoln Star', 'Etoile de Paris' or 'Viola' (a hybrid from Germany) with its minimalist four sepals, or indeed with 'Sputnik'. The attractive 'Arabella' is unsurpassed and unique among clematis in having sepals in the shape of spatulas. Looking exactly like a mini-propeller is the diminutive 'Foxtrot', whose virtues are all too often overlooked.

Large sepals

It is often surprising just how large the sepals of clematis can become through selection. Inevitably, gravity takes charge and the sepals hang down at the tips through sheer weight.

A new, smaller cultivar from Germany, 'Gizela' is very petite and dainty and led more by its large, cream boss than its reflexed sepals, which are a rich and striking, dark maroon color. 'Gizela' grows to about 3ft. (1m.) and offers its flowers most generously. The unusual qualities of

C. 'Alba Luxurians' A.G.M.
LEFT *Each flower differs in this two-tone clematis. Some have small, green patches; others are more green than white.*

C. 'Etoile de Paris'
ABOVE *With its finely pointed sepals, C. 'Etoile de Paris' demonstrates the great variety in form exhibited by the large-flowered clematis.*

C. 'Arabella'
LEFT *No other clematis has this unique shape of finely tipped, spatula-shaped sepals combined in a well-proportioned flower of firm posture.*

these clematis are simply a reflection of a powerful, natural phenomenon—variation, which is the key feature on which Charles Darwin based his natural selective theories. In the confines of the greenhouse, clematis enthusiasts can create their own unusual forms and pick their own palettes from the wide range of colors that clematis exhibit in the wild.

In nature, the pollen helps to introduce new characteristics to subsequent generations and it produces a wide variety of shape and form. Under more controlled conditions, plant breeders can exclusively introduce the pollen of one named cultivar to the female parts of another,

with a fair chance of producing some hoped-for, combined characteristics (see Propagating, pages 104–105). There is still the great opportunity of selecting something altogether unsuspected, because the genetic material in clematis pollen and ovules carries many more characters than the eye is able to see in the outward form of the parent clematis.

Pictured on these pages are several of the more exotic and outlandish-looking clematis that have extremely appealing if odd characteristics. All provide striking displays in the garden, their boldness of form insuring that they will always stand out from the crowd.

C. 'Hybrida Sieboldii'
LEFT _One of the prettiest clematis, this has a large boss and cream sepals. Flowering up a wall or pillar, it looks quite remarkable._

C. 'Gizela'
ABOVE _This cultivar has a large boss that is out of proportion with its sepals. The two colors of yellow and maroon contrast particularly well._

C. 'Pennell's Purity'
LEFT _Could this be a camellia or even a double rose perhaps? It certainly could be mistaken for either—but this beauty is indeed a pure white, double clematis._

C. 'Sputnik'
ABOVE _Typical of 'Sputnik', the sepals are elongated and wider toward the outside, all twisted in the same direction so that they resemble a whirling propeller._

Seed heads

The seeds and fruits of clematis can provide enjoyment long after the flowers have faded. Fluffy seed heads are produced in abundance, giving a delightful show once the colorful sepals have died back.

CLEMATIS MAY only flower for two weeks to a month, but the fluffy seed heads can remain on the plant for up to a year and may still be kicking around the garden or lodged in undergrowth a year after they were produced.

The structure of a typical clematis seed head (botanically called a fruit) is of many seeds inserted into the base of the flower, each with a fluffy tail designed to wing each seed to a far-off place ready for germination. As the seeds mature, the fluffiness of the pappas increases, the displays look more attractive and the plant is able to scatter its seeds to the wind.

The seed heads often complement the foliage, and they remain on the plant for some time–far longer than the flowers–while the seeds disperse; this can be seen in many hybrids and species such as *C. japonica*. The range of seed heads varies enormously, providing immense pleasure. It is a real delight to see a wall at the back of a herbaceous border covered with the fluffy heads of clematis, especially when they are caught in a shaft of sharp autumn light.

Spiky or twisted

C. orientalis and *C. tangutica* never fail to show off their autumn seeds. Sometimes the fruit head looks like a mop of fluff (as in *C. koreana* or 'Bill MacKenzie') or hangs in regimented troupes (as in *C. napaulensis*). Alternatively, it has a spiky look (*C. campaniflora*), a twisted look (*C.* 'Arabella') or a swollen base as in *C. crispa*. Whatever the variation in form, the seed heads of clematis are always an attraction in any garden.

Autumn fruits and seeds
LEFT *Goatee beards are not always this white but in old man's beard (*C. vitalba) *even the Latin name hints at its whiter than white seeds, which adorn hedges in the autumn.*

C. 'Wada's Primrose'
LEFT *Many clematis puff up their seed heads like this, and the seed is carried in the wind by the long, feathery attachments.*

C. orientalis 'Bill MacKenzie'
LEFT *A ball of fluffy seeds is typical of this popular cultivar. After the first flowers fade, a flush of seed heads appears beside new flowers.*

C. campaniflora

LEFT *Sometimes the fruit of the clematis is prettier than the flower and often it is much larger. A clematis "fruit" is the collection of seeds that develops after the flower is fertilised. The long tails attached to the clematis seeds are made up of fine hairs, which become buoyant in the air. This variant of* C. campaniflora *has wispy seed tails, unlike the similar* C. viticella, *which does not have these parts.*

C. alpina 'Francis Rivis' A.G.M.

LEFT *Fluffy balls of seed heads give this delightful appeal.*

C. macropetala

LEFT *A riot of fluffy seed heads intermingle to form a very attractive cluster.*

C. koreana

ABOVE *On tall stalks, the seed heads of this species clematis have green centers and silvery white seeds.*

CLEMATIS BY GROUP AND SEASON

C LEMATIS ARE so versatile as garden subjects that in temperate regions they can be persuaded to flower in each month of the year. Naturally there are many more that flower during their peak period from spring to summer, but there are early ones, such as the New Zealand species and cultivars and the armandiis. At the end of the year autumn-flowering flammula (the pure white clematis) can accompany the fruiting heads of *C. vitalba* or the flowers of *C. maximowicziana*. The seed heads of clematis last for a long time, making them very valuable, and the foliage of many clematis, evergreen or deciduous, is useful on its own without any flowers. It is easy to get carried away with enthusiasm for brown or bright green foliage plants in the world of clematis.

C. 'Pagoda'
ABOVE *Pagoda in shape and name, this delightfully colored clematis of viticella and patens stock flowers in mid-season.*

C. montana var. wilsonii
LEFT *This mid-summer flowerer from China is named after the early 20th-century plant collector Ernest Wilson.*

Alpina

*Hardy alpinas provide a welcome splash of early spring color, their fat
buds popping open to reveal typically blue, white or pink, bell-shaped flowers. There are many
varieties to choose from, and pruning is rarely necessary.*

ALPINAS ARE among the earliest clematis to show in the garden. I often see their parent species, the native alpinas, pushing their way through a light dusting of early-morning snow high in the mountains.

The alpinas are a hardy bunch, well-suited to the vagaries and fickleness of the weather. Spring bursts on them so quickly that once the plump, little flower buds form, it is only a matter of days before they pop open to welcome spring and the arrival of pollinating honey bees. Indeed, they can make a huge splash of color up a wall or in a container on a patio shortly after New Year. Since alpinas need little or no pruning, at least until they are established five- to six-year-old plants, they belong to pruning group 1 (see pages 102-103).

For alpinas, read hundreds of little flowers on a two-year-old plant. There is no stinting in flower production, unlike some hybrids, which produce rationings of a couple of flowers now and two later on. One of the better characteristics of alpinas is that they hardly ever need pruning. With more than 20 known alpina hybrids there is a great variety to choose from. They broadly have the same

C. alpina 'Pink Flamingo'
ABOVE *These pretty clematis show
off their pinkness to great effect
whenever the flowers nod in
the wind.*

C. alpina 'Helsingborg' A.G.M.
LEFT *The dark purple sepals, which
have a definite sleek quality,
contrast well with the bright
green foliage.*

**C. alpina subsp. sibirica
'White Moth'**
RIGHT *The sepals of this sub-species
open out like wings (resembling a
white moth, hence the name) to
show off a white-green boss.*

structure, that is they have bell-shaped flowers with rather pointed sepals, but they differ in size, color and refinements of their various parts. Pinks, blues and whites are very typical.

'Pink Flamingo' has a special crustacean-rose color to it and looks grand *en masse*. Both 'Ruby' and 'Tage Lundell' are pink, while the popular 'Willy' has a touch of blue with its pinkness. 'Constance', 'Frankie' and 'Mrs T. Lundell' keep the pinkness, but the blues are represented by such beauties as the broad-sepaled 'Frankie' or the sleek 'Columbine'.

There is a particularly fine, white form of the latter—'White Columbine' A.G.M.—which, even though a departure from the pinkness of alpinas, is certainly a match for the wider-flowered subspecies of *C.a.* subsp. *sibirica* 'White Moth'. A good example of how selection has changed the structure of the clematis that we are all familiar with is *C.a.* 'Francis Rivis' A.G.M. This is a pale blue-colored alpina but it has diverged into two different stocks. The first—'Francis Rivis'—is now known as the Dutch stock, from which a longer-petaled stock became known in England as the U.K. stock.

There are some who believe that the long-sepaled 'Blue Dancer' is the same as 'Francis Rivis' Dutch stock. If ever there was an over-enthusiastic grower it is 'Blue Dancer', which can reward with hundreds of flowers on a single plant that last for a month in the spring.

C. alpina 'Frankie'
ABOVE *The short sepals are well-proportioned and enclose a boss of pale green stamens.*

C. alpina 'Jacqueline du Pré'
LEFT *The subtle color tones of pink and mauve vary from top to underside and there is a characteristic, pale edge to the underside of the sepals.*

C. alpina **'White Columbine' A.G.M.**
LEFT *Hanging in white splendor (as opposed to pale blue in the 'Columbine' form), the sepals are twice as long as the central boss area and they combine very well with their green foliage.*

DIFFERENCES IN STRUCTURE

The short and the long of it (with apologies to William Shakespeare) is that the UK form of 'Francis Rivis' is long and the Dutch form, from which it was derived, is short. The two forms have diverged to such a degree that they now look like entirely different plants.

C. alpina 'Francis Rivis' (Dutch form) A.G.M.
Short, wavy sepals are seen in the original form from Holland, which looks like a robust flower with a large boss.

C. alpina 'Francis Rivis' A.G.M.
Here the sepals are elongated but they have kept their wavy edges. The flower now has a certain elegance.

C. alpina 'Blue Dancer'
Through selection the boss has become longer and more pronounced and the sepals have become very long with a certain twist in them.

Macropetala

*These small-sized clematis flowers have long, thin sepals and are at their best
in late spring to early summer. As vines, they can grow up to three or four yards, which
makes it possible to look up into the flowers and enjoy their massed beauty.*

LIKE ALPINAS, macropetalas are small-sized clematis, also grouped as atrogenes, thus an old name was *Atragene macropetala*. The atragene group also includes such species as *C. koreana, C. chiisanensis* and *C. ochotensis*. The flowers are, as the name reflects almost correctly, 'large petaled'. The numerous long, thin sepals are joined by several stamenoids from the central boss. In the true species the flowers are quite large, about 2in. (5cm.) across, and are nodding.

The macropetalas flower from late spring to early summer, generally just after the alpinas, and some may flower again in the autumn. They belong to pruning group 1, so need virtually no pruning (see pages 102-103). Among the later spring-flowering macropetalas are 'Lagoon' (formerly called 'Blue Lagoon'), which retains the large flower of the native species but is a deep violet-blue, and 'Floralia', which is smaller and a delicate pale pink. 'Floralia' is a recent hybrid from Sweden, bred from parents *C. macropetala* and *C. ochotensis*. The shape of the flowers has influenced the naming of the different types, such as the purple-pink 'Purple Spider' or the palest pink 'Ballet Skirt'. Two macropetalas have A.G.M. status: 'Markham's Pink' A.G.M., a pink form which looks otherwise like the true species; and 'Maidwell Hall' A.G.M., which is violet in color. There are other macropetala types that have in recent years been removed from their close association with macropetalas, although they share some genetic material. They include 'White Moth' and 'White Swan', but the former was moved in 1997 to be part of the alpinas (as *C. alpina* subsp. *sibirica* 'White Moth'), the latter to stand alone as a separate cultivar. 'Rosie O'Grady' is a pale pink form, which may have more in common with alpinas than macropetalas. Confusion remains over the names of the atrogene alpinas and macropetalas, because *C. alpina* 'Constance' looks rather like a macropetala but is with the alpinas.

***C. macropetala* 'White Swan'**
ABOVE *The degree to which the sepals are fluffed up and divided to give this analagous effect of a swan's downy back is typical of macropetalas.*

***C. macropetala* 'Lagoon'**
LEFT *The beauty of macropetalas is their penchant for multi-sepaled displays, as here in "Lagoon".*

MACROPETALA SPECIES

Macropetalas have robust, multi-sepaled flowers that are borne in large numbers on a vigorous rootstock. *En masse*, they make a great backdrop and there are a number of subdued color tones that are useful in any garden. This species clematis has a mass of pointed sepals radiating out from the center. The flowers have a soft, downy appearance as a result of tiny hairs and persist for some time in late spring.

C. macropetala 'Purple Spider'
ABOVE *A spidery effect is created by long, wavy sepals in this purple-flowered macropetala.*

C. macropetala

C. macropetala 'Ballet Skirt'
LEFT *The manner in which the elongated and pointed sepals are dispersed in this variety has given rise to its name. This is an old specimen which has lost its deep pink color.*

Montana

*The garden would be a far less pretty place if it were not for montanas, which
owe their relative hardiness to their origins in the Himalayas and central and western China.
They are phenomenal climbers and rampant growers.*

T HE MONTANAS do well in an English climate but are not always hardy in Scandinavia or North America. In the 19th century only two such clematis were being recommended for gardens, according to A. Ysabeau (1874) in 'Le Jardinier', one of these seemed to be a clematis montana 'la clématite odorante', the other 'la clématite d'Henderson'.

Spring is the time for montanas and an established plant can push through the canopies of substantial trees or emerge from the impenetrability of a hedge with showers of white, pink or red-pink flowers. Their powers as climbers, or strong vines, is phenomenal and, as deciduous plants, they can surprise gardeners with their rampant growth. It is not unusual for a pot-bought montana to double its size within a month, and flower, too. There is simplicity to the flowers of montana, which are based on just four sepals. Their stunning effects in the garden are entirely due to their magnificent floriferous nature. Montanas belong to pruning group 1, so they need little or no pruning (see pages 102-103).

Distinctive montanas

One of the more distinctive montanas is the Wilson's anemone clematis, or Wilson's mountain clematis, which is often known as *C.m.* var. *wilsonii.* This has fairly spiky, white sepals with a central, cream boss of anthers. There is of course a double—as you might expect from any wild plant—which is *C.m.* 'Marjorie': this has a peculiar shade of stripy reddish pink as if splashed in paint, and this combination is virtually unique in the clematis world. In consequence, 'Marjorie' does look stunning grown over an arbor. There are many

C. montana var. *wilsonii'*
LEFT *Quite distinctive among the montanas, this* wilsonii *variety is characterised by short and narrow sepals that are twisted around their axis. The effect is unusual and can make some flowers look like butterflies in flight.*

C. montana 'Mrs. Margaret Jones'

LEFT *Two unusual characteristics of this plant are that it does not have any stamens and that it is suffused with green. Introduced in 1991, it has semi-double, star-like flowers, which appear in mid-spring.*

C. montana 'Spooneri'

ABOVE *The flowers are very uniform with broad, white sepals surrounding a whirl of yellow stamens. It is a strong grower and will attain 33ft. (10m.) in height.*

C. montana var. sericea A.G.M.

LEFT *A very prolific flowerer, this plant has large sepals, somewhat overlapping, with wavy edges. Like most montanas, it is vigorous.*

different types of montanas, and many seedlings of unknown parentage to confuse those who wish to identify them. Among these many pink montanas are the palest pinks of 'Pink Perfection' or 'Elizabeth' A.G.M., a pinker pink of 'Mayleen' or a richer pink of 'Picton's Variety'. Small pink flowers and pink stems are typical of 'Warwickshire Rose', while the large flowers of typical montanas are retained along with bronze foliage in 'Vera' and 'Freda' A.G.M.—the latter having the richest pink sepals of all montanas. It was raised by Jim Fisk in Suffolk, England in 1985.

For prolonged growth try *C.m.* 'Continuity', which, as its name suggests, has a fairly continuous flowering period from early spring through to late summer. It has one disadvantage in that it is very difficult to propagate, because it has hollow stems. Montanas are not generally very scented, but 'Fragrant Spring', 'Mayleen' and 'Vera' all have some scent—the latter two emanating a vanilla fragrance.

C. montana 'Freda' A.G.M.
ABOVE *The large pink flowers contrast well with the dark foliage. With such attractive color combinations, this plant makes a useful addition to any garden against a wall or on a trellis.*

C. montana 'Continuity'
LEFT *Of all the montanas, this is one that flowers right through from spring to autumn, and, as its name suggests, it brings color for several months. It is a powerful grower and will cover sheds.*

C. montana 'Mayleen'
LEFT *The flowers have a crumpled look and are pink without any scent. The sepals are short and reflexed a little at extremities, and the boss is large. The plant is vigorous, can be grown in any aspect and has dark foliage.*

C. montana 'Picton's Variety'
RIGHT *The sepals are rounder and of a darker pink than those of 'Elizabeth'. The flowers are scented and the plant is vigorous, up to 33ft. (10m.).*

Early hybrids

*These are hybrids that flower after the spring clematis, in late spring or early summer,
and before the late-flowering hybrids. They flower on last year's
wood and may be singles or doubles.*

ALL EARLY-FLOWERING hybrids owe their parentage to the Chinese native *C. patens*. This is a white- to light purplish-blue-flowered clematis with brown or purple-brown anthers. There is an elusive, blue form, too, which may not now exist in the wild. There are various Japanese and Chinese forms of patens and there are multi-sepaled, double cultivars, such as 'Yukiokoshi' and 'Ruriokosh'.

It is well to be reminded that William Robinson loathed doubles and would immediately burn them if they appeared in his garden. He thought them totally unfit for the rigors of the English climate. His was a very personal view. I disagree. I think that doubles have a great deal of charisma and are enormously under-rated. The wide variety in color and form exhibited in *C. patens* is translated into the wide variety of colors and forms seen in early-flowering hybrids. One of the most familiar in gardens is *C.* 'Wada's Primrose', which may actually be a form of *C. patens*.

All the early-flowered hybrids are deciduous and have attractive seed heads. They also belong to pruning group 2, since they flower on the previous years' wood (see pages 102–103). Their flowers are large and the plants are generally compact on stems that can reach up to 10ft. (3m.). Some might have a second or even a third flush of flowers well into the autumn. Hybrids such as 'Horn of Plenty' or 'Ivan Olsson' are repeat-flowering. They make excellent subjects in containers (such hybrids as 'Joan Picton', 'Kacper', 'Natacha' and 'Ruby Glow' are typical), and some of them are scented, such as 'Lady Londesborough', which hints of violets.

C. 'Jackmanii Alba'
ABOVE *A vigorous hybrid, this has larger flowers in early summer and smaller ones later on.*

C. 'Alice Fisk'
LEFT *With its bright wisteria-blue color, this cultivar has pointed and crenulated sepals. It flowers first in early summer and again later on.*

C. 'Ville de Lyon'

LEFT *A good scrambler if left alone, 'Ville de Lyon' will often surprise the unwary gardener with shots of color just where they are not expected.*

C. 'Satsukibare'

RIGHT *Strident in its red-purples, this early clematis comes out in late spring to early summer and makes a good display.*

C. 'Joan Picton'

ABOVE *Full-bodied and freshly pink with a smidgeon of blushing, this is a particularly fine specimen of the popular cultivar.*

C. 'Comtesse de Bouchaud' A.G.M.

LEFT *A prolific flowerer, this is useful for color matching from early summer, its pink hue combining well with many other species.*

Late species and hybrids

These are clematis that flower in mid- to late summer and in the autumn. They flower on the current season's new growth and include many large-flowered cultivars, species clematis, the viticellas and the tanguticas.

A S THESE clematis flower on the current season's new growth, they belong to pruning group 3 (see pages 102–103). After flowering in late autumn they can be roughly pruned, to safeguard the plant during the winter storms, and then be pruned seriously back to two buds in early spring. That way the plant is less likely to succumb to infection in cut or split stems during inclement weather.

Members of the tangutica groups do not need any pruning, because they are well used to growing up pillars and walls, continuing in the same vein in following years. All they need is some heavy pruning from time to time to cut out too much dense growth.

Viticellas, such as 'Alba Luxurians' A.G.M., 'Blue Belle' and 'Venosa Violacea' A.G.M., have as a parent the native species, *C. viticella*, from southern Europe and western Asia. It bears single flowers, which may be blue, purple or rose-purple, and these color characteristics have expressed themselves in the many exciting hybrids and cultivars that exist. Viticellas are excellent for growing through herbaceous plants and shrubs or up over arches, arbors or gazebos. They finger their way through other hosts to make delightful displays. Among popular varieties are 'Etoile Violette' A.G.M., 'Polish Spirit' A.G.M., 'Purpurea Plena Elegans' A.G.M. and 'Royal Velours' A.G.M.

Many species clematis flower at the same time as late hybrids, which means that the two can be grown together very successfully. The species are good value, since they are generally reliable, relatively resistant to disease and mostly floriferous. They have come to the clematis garden from around the world: *chinensis, connata, florida, ladakhiana* from China (though *C. florida* appears to have now disappeared from the wild), *flammula* from southern Europe, *integrifolia* and *orientalis* from eastern Europe. From the Himalayas we have *gouriana* and *grata*, while from North America have come *ligusticifolia* and *pitcheri*. Some, such as *apiifolia, brachiata* and *flammula*, are scented.

C. 'Emilia Plater'
ABOVE *Showing off its viticella heritage, this purple-mauve masterpiece has reflexed sepals.*

C. 'Jackmanii' A.G.M.
LEFT *Bright and beautiful, cheap and cheerful, this very popular cultivar has become a classic clematis, ideal for welcoming in a long, hot summer.*

C. 'Elsa Späth' A.G.M.
LEFT *The sculptured sepals of this appealing cultivar have curvaceous and evocative lines, which can be seen from mid- to late summer.*

C. 'Rouge Cardinal'
ABOVE *Deep red in color, dignified to the status of a red-cloaked cardinal, this popular cultivar grows well during summer against a wall, up a tripod or on a trellis.*

C. 'Madame Baron Veillard'
ABOVE *Deliciously pink, this cultivar comes out from late summer through to autumn and has nicely formed sepals that give a uniform shape to the flower.*

Large-flowered hybrids

*Big is always beautiful in clematis, not least among the largest of them all—
the large-flowered clematis. Indeed a sizable display of large-flowered plants can
sometimes defy description, if not gravity.*

ONE WOULD be forgiven for thinking that clematis breeders have a single-track mind in selecting only big and beautiful clematis. Starting only with native species and the generous sports they usually throw up, such as albinos, doubles and those with frilly sepals, there has nevertheless been a tendency to produce some very large-flowered hybrids—at an expense. Not all breeders think big. There are plenty of other clematis hybrids that are small and beautiful and have their own special virtues.

Many, if not most, of the large-flowered clematis are in fact mauve to purple in color as the following pages indicate. It is a question of how large is "large-flowered". "Dinner-plate" clematis is another term used to refer to clematis, and that is the size being looked at here, among which are such clematis as 'Boskoop Beauty' up to 8¼in. (21cm.),

'Kacper', 'Kathleen Wheeler' and 'Liberation' up to 9in. (23cm.) or 'Fairy Queen' up to 10in. (25cm.).

'Fairy Queen', as one of the largest hybrids known, has been around for over 100 years, since it was raised by Cripps & Sons in England in 1875. My own plant produces flowers up to 8¼ in. (21cm.) and is often wont to "drop" two big flower buds and put all its energies into a single fine blossom—two buds flopping over and wasting away in favor of one large flower. Its delicate pink bars along the white-with-a-suffusion-of-pink sepals are distinctly attractive, such colors being fit for any fairy queen.

The term "large-flowered" clematis is often interpreted by authors as being any clematis larger than 'Niobe' A.G.M. or 'Carnaby'—or about 4in. (10cm.) in diameter. However, if one looks at the largest selection of clematis known, of more

C. 'Saturn'
RIGHT *The huge sepals are distinguished by delicate hues.*

C. 'Edouard Desfossé'
LEFT *Falling back at the edges, this magnificent cultivar has a striking boss area centralised within its mauve flowers.*

C. 'Fairy Queen'
ABOVE *White and pink sepals make this a striking clematis, which is easy to grow in the garden, perhaps up an old apple tree stump.*

than 6in. (15cm.), then it removes smaller ones such as the pink 'John Warren', 'Twilight' and 'Helen Cropper' or the dark purples such as 'Warszawska Nike' or 'Niobe' A.G.M. and all the jackmanii plants.

One of the characteristics of the really large clematis is that their sepals are sometimes overcome by gravity and start to droop: see particularly 'Saturn', 'Edouard Desfossé' or 'Kathleen Wheeler'. This is hardly surprising, since a 10in. (25cm.) diameter flower would support about 195sq.in. (490sq.cm.) of surface area of sepal—more in those cases where the sepals overlap, such as 'W.E. Gladstone'. It is

surprising nonetheless that the large-flowered clematis (in general) often do support such a large surface of sepal, and, in those cases (most) that do not droop, the alignment of the sepals is all on one horizontal plane.

The perfection of the clematis flower is indeed a wonder, since side-on the sepals are as thin as a knife blade. Dinner-plate-sized clematis are always welcome in any garden and often come as a big surprise. Some, such as 'Evening Star', may be susceptible to sudden wilt; others to wind damage or drooping, because of their large size; but given their considerable attributes, this is a very small price to pay.

C. 'Evening Star'
LEFT *On the medium to large side, these clematis are bright and colorful and make a feature in any border.*

C. 'W.E. Gladstone'
LEFT *Large and wide, the sepals overlap to create an impressive dinner-plate effect, signed off with a dark center.*

C. 'Kathleen Wheeler'
ABOVE *With a contrasting center, this has large sepals that are reflexed at their tips.*

Viticella

This is an exciting group of clematis, exhibiting diversity in color while retaining its characteristic bell-shaped, nodding flowers. Viticellas make excellent plants for growing over arbors, arches and posts and through bedding and foliage plants.

LIKE THE montanas, the viticellas are a large group of clematis that have today been selected into many different cultivars. *C. viticella* is a native wild plant of southern Europe through to western Asia and is a scrambling vine to about 10ft. (3m.). It has small, blue, purple or rose-purple flowers. A valuable garden plant, it is best to see it bloom before buying from a garden center or nursery, because the quality of the flowers varies.

C. viticella was originally introduced to England in the 16th century, when it was known as the Virgin's bower in honor of Queen Elizabeth I, a name also used to describe other native clematis species both sides of the Atlantic. Viticellas usually produced flowers in great abundance on a substantial plant. They have the added virtue of being resistant to wilt, and make excellent plants for growing over arbors, arches, posts, walls and through other plants including bedding and foliage plants, such as heaths.

They are moderately vigorous, so are not difficult to keep under control. They flower from mid-summer through to autumn, their nodding bells being a source of enduring delight for any gardener. Since viticellas belong to pruning group 3, they are best pruned hard in early spring (see pages 102-103).

C. 'Etoile Violette' A.G.M.
ABOVE *One attraction of viticellas is the way that their small flowers nod in the breeze. Another is their color, which in this example is quite characteristic.*

C. viticella
LEFT *The small, nodding, purple heads of viticella are typical of this species clematis and are about 2in. (5cm.) long. The sepals have ridges running along their length.*

C. 'Minuet' A.G.M.
RIGHT *A delightful variety, 'Minuet' has little flowers that are mauve on the outside and green inside, and green stamens. It grows well in a herbaceous border.*

Prolific numbers of double flowers always appear on *C. viticella* 'Purpurea Plena Elegans' A.G.M., another old cultivar from the 16th century. Its vigorous growth is best focused on arches and arbors, where it can smother the sides and roof with its magnificent mass of flowers.

Larger viticellas are seen in 'Polish Spirit' A.G.M., which was raised by Brother Stefan in Poland and has large, rich purple-blue flowers, or in the extraordinary *C.* 'Alba Luxurians' A.G.M., which is in a class of its own—like 'Purpurea Plena Elegans' A.G.M. in terms of uniqueness of flower shape and color combination. *C.* 'Alba Luxurians' A.G.M. makes quick work of a fence or wall, which it can readily cover with flowers.

Viticellas are extremely dainty, small flowers that are produced in large numbers. At their best they can grow as thickets over arbors in the space of a few years. Purples, reds, maroons and violet colors are all expressed through the vibrant world of viticellas, and all gardens should have some of them.

Today's viticella hybrids have other clematis species "blood" in them, such as *C.* x *eriostemon*, which was originally produced from a cross between *C. viticella* and *C. integrifolia* in 1837.

HYBRIDISATION
Dutch breeders in about 1830 are believed to have brought together *C. viticella* and *C. integrifolia* to produce the similarly colored hybrid *C.* x. *eriostemon*.

C. viticella

C. integrifolia

C. x *eriostemon*

C. 'Margot Koster'
LEFT *This plant produces masses of mauve-pink flowers. It likes the sun and will grow up to 10ft. (3m.) on a fence or pillar.*

C. 'Abundance'
LEFT *The rose-pink flowers are relatively small and compact, with the sepals slightly recurved at their ends. The stamens are greenish.*

C. viticella 'Purpurea Plena Elegans' A.G.M.
LEFT *This double-flowered clematis is believed to be an old European cultivar, dating from the 16th century.*

C. 'Madame Julia Correvon' A.G.M.
RIGHT *Large, single flowers are produced on a vigorous vine that does well up a pillar, tripod or high fence.*

Texensis

Nearly all texensis clematis have tulip-shaped flowers, which are either nodding or gracefully upstanding. They can make a wonderfully colorful display on a garden wall, since they flower prolifically from a naturally vigorous rootstock.

TEXENSIS CLEMATIS are derived from the wild species *C. texensis*, which is native to Texas in the United States. Its old Latin name of *C. coccinea* describes the color of the sepals, which in the wild species vary from scarlet to purple-red. The color of the species texensis is very bright, almost a red-orange, in the form of a small tulip-shaped flower with a yellow-white throat.

This characteristic red color has been kept in most of the cultivars so far produced, though it comes as a delicate pink in *C.* 'Duchess of Albany' A.G.M. or a softer red in *C.* 'Etoile Rose'. Strident red is seen in *C.* 'Gravetye Beauty', more so on the inside of the sepals than on the outside. The farthest deviation from the color of the texensis species is seen in *C.* 'Pagoda', which has purple stripes on the underside, edged in white. The shape of the texensis cultivars

has changed little, except in *C.* 'Pagoda', whose name describes the upturned ends of the sepals. Typical of the texensis group is *C.* 'Princess of Wales'. A clematis of this name was produced in the 1890s and nearly 90 years later Barry Fretwell introduced a similar variety called 'The Princess of Wales'. By convention, it has to be called by its original name and not its other name of 'Princess Diana'. Texensis hybrids are well worth growing in the garden. Their green and blue-green foliage is produced prolifically, like the flowers, and individual plants can reach 10ft. (3m.). They die back to the ground each year. Since they belong to pruning group 3, dead stems can be cut back after flowering but hard pruning should not take place until spring. Although resistant to clematis wilt, they are susceptible to fungal attack from mildew.

C. 'Etoile Rose'
ABOVE *This offspring of a texensis parent has delicately nodding flowers, reflexed at the tips, a yellow-cream boss and green foliage.*

C. 'Gravetye Beauty'
LEFT *Another popular variety, this has wide open, firm red flowers, which grow on a vine with abundant energy.*

C. 'Princess of Wales'
RIGHT *This favored hybrid has many texensis genes and produces perfectly shaped, upright, tulip-like flowers with pale insides.*

Orientalis and tangutica

In general terms, this group of clematis look much the same and grow in a similar fashion. They all come from Iran, the Himalayas and China and there are species, natural clones and cultivars among them.

THERE IS some confusion surrounding the classification of orientalis, tangutica and tibetana clematis. As with many contentious issues of classification there are the "lumpers", who put all similar species into one group, and the "splitters", who make separate species. I prefer separate species but am wary of man-made classification as nature never fits tidily into it.

If we adopt one early way of interpretation, tanguticas are within a section of orientalis clematis. In this classification there are 10 clematis that fall within the orientalis section: *C. akebioides, C. graveolens, C. hilariae, C. intricata, C. ladakhiana, C. orientalis, C. pamiralaica, C. serratifolia, C. tangutica* and *C. tibetana*. They can be lumped together, or treated as distinct species. As listed they are shown as species, yet there are others, such as *C. tibetana* subsp. *vernayi* A.G.M. or *C. tangutica* 'Radar Love', that are popular subspecies and cultivars respectively—the latter comes with a guarantee to flower three months from setting seed, reflecting the vigorous nature of the section. Within this section the plants have green or glaucous leaves, with simple, lobed, toothed or untoothed leaflets, and yellow or yellow-green flowers that are belled, lantern or reflexed. There is a tendency to call all yellow-belled clematis 'Orange Peel' clematis, but strictly this is a cultivar name of *C. tangutica*.

The most celebrated person associated with this group is William MacKenzie (1904–1995), who had a new cultivar named after him, *C. tangutica* 'Bill MacKenzie'.

C. tangutica 'Bill MacKenzie'
ABOVE *Having the fluffy seed heads and the flowers together on the plant at the same time is very typical of this clematis and adds to its appeal.*

LEFT *Shown here growing at Waterperry Gardens in Oxfordshire, England, 'Bill MacKenzie' can be expected to grow to these proportions against or over a wall at the back of a herbaceous border. It is rampant and after a while will tend to flower at the top in the sunshine rather than down below. Judicious pruning may encourage it to perform lower down.*

C. orientalis

LEFT *The thick, shiny sepals are a much sought-after quality of this species clematis.*

C. orientalis hort, now tibetana

LEFT *In apparent regimental form, the flower heads hang down in typical fashion, with their flower parts tucked up inside and accessible to pollinating insects.*

C. tangutica 'Helios'

ABOVE *Looking just like a propeller, the sepals of 'Helios' are particularly attractive.*

C. tibetana subsp. vernayi A.G.M.

LEFT *Lost in a flurry of yellow sepals and flower parts, the form of this plant is less distinct.*

C. tangutica 'Orange Peel'

ABOVE *'Orange Peel' is specific to this variety but is also a general term that applies to many of the tanguticas.*

Herbaceous clematis

*Herbaceous clematis make a great contribution to color in a
herbaceous border. They die down during winter but emerge with upright stems
and large leaves in the spring.*

ERBACEOUS CLEMATIS make an interesting diversion from the normal climbing or clinging clematis, since they are upright, or—more often—floppy plants that need staking or rely on other plants for support and they can be deployed to great effect in the herbaceous border. The vigor is still there, and some will grow from nothing by about a yard within a few weeks. In autumn they die down to ground level.

Heracleifolias

Heracleifolias are herbaceous perennial clematis with tubular flowers, recalling their old name of *C. tubulosa*, with four sepals reflexed back on themselves. Young plants can look a little ungainly but a mature patch can become quite rampant and occupy a useful part of the border, contributing good foliage punctuated with mauve and purple flowers from a range of hybrids. They can make sprawling ground cover, or they can produce light thickets of thousands of flowers. Among just a handful of heracleifolias there is only one that is an A.G.M.—*C. heracleifolia* 'Wyevale', which has light blue flowers and firm, upright leaves. Other popular varieties are 'Côte d'Azur' and 'Campanile'. There are other herbaceous clematis that are closely related, and these include *C. x jouiniana* 'Mrs. Robert Brydon', which has white to pale mauve flowers—the parent of this hybrid being *C. heracleifolia*. *C. x jouiniana* used to be known as *C. grata*, and there are a number of varieties that foam with flowers and are expansive in their colonisation of the herbaceous border when mature.

Scents are characteristic of a number of heracleifolias and *x jouiniana* hybrids, although they may be subtle and unnoticed. *C. heracleifolia* var.

***C. heracleifolia* 'Côte d'Azur'**
LEFT *This has pale blue, unscented flowers and large leaves and is a cross with 'Campanile' (right).*

***C. x jouiniana* 'Mrs. Robert Brydon'**
LEFT *This herbaceous plant has clusters of off-white flowers, which are scented. The leaves are large and coarse.*

***C. heracleifolia* 'Campanile'**
ABOVE *Pale blue flowers are borne from the base of the large leaves of this herbaceous plant.*

heracleifolia is scented, so too are the dried leaves of *C.h.* var. *davidiana*. Other scented herbaceous clematis include *C. recta* 'Peveril' and *C. koreana* var. *fragrans*, which smells of cedarwood.

Integrifolias

Like heracleifolias, the leaves of integrifolias are dark green and provide useful foliage, especially when grown as a clump in a herbaceous border. Typical flowers of integrifolia are bell-shaped with upturned sepals, varying from pale pink through to blue, and flowering from mid-summer to the autumn. Of the dozen or so types of integrifolia, there is a single true species of *C. integrifolia*, which is a native of Europe and Asia, blue being the typical color. This is one of the earliest to have been introduced to Britain, coming from eastern Europe in 1573. Different types of integrifolia tend to vary in the hue of blue or pink, there being just one A.G.M. plant listed—'Rosea' A.G.M.—which has a strong pink color. Nearly all integrifolias are recognised by their reflexed sepals and bell-like characters, but 'Olgae' differs in having much wider sepals without any of the bell-like attributes. One of the most delicate integrifolias is 'Pastel Pink', with its long, wispy sepals of pale pink-purple. One of the smallest flowers is 'Alba', with its white, reflexed bells. Among the blues, the hybrid *C.* x *eriostemon* 'Hendersonii' has the darkest flowers of the integrifolias, with strongly reflexed sepals sporting a proportionately large boss of cream anthers.

Another popular and widespread herbaceous border plant, derived from integrifolias but not always listed with them, is *C.* x *durandii* A.G.M. A hybrid, *C.* x *durandii* A.G.M. has large, bluish sepals with distinctive ribs. It has not quite lost the reflexed nature of the sepals but the flowers appear open and they stand up, rather than hang down as bells.

C. integrifolia
LEFT *For growers who are looking for a herbaceous species clematis, integrifolia offers attractive, pale purple, nodding heads and cream and white stamens.*

C. integrifolia hybrid
ABOVE *This pretty contender has wide, pale pink sepals with a deeper pink bar.*

C. x **durandii A.G.M.**
LEFT *One of the most valuable clematis for a herbaceous border, this is upstanding to $1^1/_2$ ft. (0.5m.). It needs nearby plants for support to show off its blue flowers to the full.*

C. integrifolia 'Pangbourne Pink'
ABOVE *The flowers on this plant are a pale pink, but otherwise it is the same as the species integrifolia.*

New Zealand clematis

There is a small outpost of native clematis in New Zealand that do not look like typical clematis and are often not recognised as such. These are not true climbers but will liven up any windowbox, hanging basket or container during the summer.

THE NEW ZEALAND species all have small, white, cream or greenish flowers and their leaflets are finely divided and often evergreen. The small plants show typical buttercup family (*Ranunculaceae*) characteristics, their flowers recalling the shape and arrangement of pheasant's eye (*Adonis annua*) and the divided leaves recalling monkshood (*Aconitum napellus*).

In their natural habitat the New Zealand clematis are typical alpine species and grow in nooks and crannies in mountainous areas. The general definition of an "alpine" species is any plant that grows above 3,000ft. (1,000m.). *C. marmoraria* A.G.M. was discovered in 1970 at 4,350ft. (1,450m.)

and is the smallest of the New Zealand species. All these are endemic to New Zealand.

Outside their native country, the New Zealand species are usually grown as alpines in greenhouses, but they can be brought through winter successfully in southern temperate regions. They also survive outside in urban areas where the year-round minimum winter temperature is up to 7°F (4°C) higher than in the countryside. When not flowering they can look rather scruffy, but their clematis interest overrides any temporary dullness.

There are 11 species of New Zealand clematis and all have separate male and female plants (dioecious). Many have evergreen foliage and one,

C. marmoraria A.G.M.
ABOVE *As a male plant, this has typical features of small, white or cream flowers borne on much-divided foliage. The sepals are firm and relatively glossy.*

C. 'Joanna'
ABOVE *This female cultivar has slightly larger flowers than* C. marmoraria *but the key feature is the verdant green center of the flower. The foliage is much the same, more like a ranunculus than a clematis.*

C. 'Pixie'
LEFT *The sepals on this male plant are rather elliptical and pointed and have a pale green hue. The stamens make a firm bunch and are yellowish.*

C. afoliata, has fragrant flowers. In the wild the seed of these New Zealand species breeds true, but when grown in cultivation many different clones are produced. One such clone that arose from seed of *C. marmoraria* sent to Scotland was *C.* x *cartmanii* 'Joe', which has flowers twice the size. There is much confusion over Latin names, since some of the original species names have now been lumped together, such as *C. petriei, C. australis* and *C. hookeriana* with *C. forsteri*.

The 'County Park Hybrids' clematis all originate from County Park Nursery in Hornchurch, Essex, England. This is run by Tony Hutchins, who travels extensively in New Zealand introducing many new varieties to the trade. His nursery has perhaps the largest collection of antipodean plants available in the northern hemisphere and Tony has been responsible for introducing such delights as 'Pixie'

(male), 'Fairy' (female), 'Green Velvet' (male), 'Moonman' (male) and 'Lunar Lass' (female) as well as 'Joanna' (female), which was launched in 1997 and named after his granddaughter.

Although the flowers of the New Zealand species and cultivars look fairly similar in color and size, there are finer differences that separate them. The number of sepals is variable from five to eight, so this is not always a good point for identification, and they may be rounded or pointed. The central boss is usually quite large in proportion to the sepals, and a greenish hue is seen in *C. indivisa*, 'Joanna' and *C.* x *cartmanii*. These antipodean delights are well worth growing in a very small garden, in an alpine border or a series of containers. They do not need much space and there is something to see on them year-round in temperate climes. Their finely divided foliage is quite unlike that of any other clematis.

C. afoliata x *forsteri*
LEFT *The flowers of this female hybrid are small and yellowish with a yellow center of stamens and a ring of yellow sepals almost in the form of a semi-double flower.*

C. afoliata
ABOVE *This is a vigorous but rather tender female clematis, named* afoliata *because it has tiny, reduced leaves. It photosynthesises using pigments in its green stem, and tiny flowers pop out from buds along the stem.*

C. forsteri
ABOVE *A female clematis, this has characteristically green, oval and smooth leaves. The small, white flowers have pointed white sepals. It is not vigorous and does well in a container.*

Polish clematis

The city center of Warsaw in Poland may seem an unlikely location for breeding clematis—yet some remarkable hybrids come from a monastery there. These have been raised by Brother Stefan Franczak and are noted for their color and diversity.

DURING THE summer of 1997 while researching this book, I had the happy experience of visiting Brother Stefan Franczak in Warsaw, Poland. Brother Stefan has spent much of his life breeding clematis, as well as day-lilies, in the city's Jesuit monastery. He has raised at least 18 named hybrids, some of which are now well-known around the world. It takes him several years to breed a new hybrid, selecting them for their beauty, hardiness and disease resistance.

The new clematis Brother Stefan produces are often named after episodes of struggle or difficulty endured by the Polish people over the years, particularly during the occupation. 'Polish Spirit' A.G.M. and 'Monte Cassino', for example, recall the successful battle fought by Polish forces at the Italian monastery of Monte Cassino during the Second World War. *C.* 'Warszawska Nike' is a popular clematis that reflects the allegorical figure of a half-fish, half-woman depicted in the Heroes of Warsaw monument in that city.

The bright red clematis 'Kardynal Wyszyński' is named after the Archbishop of Warsaw, Cardinal Stefan Wysinsk (1901–1981), who was imprisoned by the Communists in 1953. His tomb may be seen in the Cathedral of Gniezno. Bred by Brother Stefan it was introduced to Britain by Jim Fisk in 1989. *C.* 'Jadwiga Teresa' (sometimes spelt 'Matka Teresa') is also another introduction by Brother Stefan, which, according to Raymond Evison, is in fact *C.* 'Général Sikorski' A.G.M.—an identical-looking clematis. Both Jim Fisk and Raymond Evison received 'Général Sikorski' A.G.M. at the same time from Wladyslaw Noll in Warsaw and Jim Fisk introduced it to the British public in 1980. Wladyslaw Noll died in 1986.

New hybrids

Some of the new hybrids that are currently being raised by Brother Stefan are shown on these pages. They are known only as code numbers such as '438–95', which refers to the selection 438 made in 1995. Brother Stefan takes about 10 years to prepare a hybrid for release, since he tries them out in different conditions, for instance in full sun, in the shade and away from the wind. The range of color and diversity among the clematis he produces has to be admired.

New in 1997 from Brother Stefan were 'Siostra Faustyna Kowalska', named after Sister Maria Faustina (1905–1938), who was made a saint in 1997 by Pope John Paul II. The Polish pope himself is remembered in *C.* 'Jan Pawel II', which was introduced to the trade by Jim Fisk in 1981. I was privileged to be given *C.* 'Pietr Skarga' by Brother Stefan when I left Warsaw and can certainly confirm the vibrancy of this new, deep violet-blue hybrid.

Brother Stefan's garden
ABOVE *In an enclosed quadrangle of a monastery in the center of Warsaw, Brother Stefan gardens with no fertilisers. Instead he uses sticks and home-produced compost—by looking after the roots, the plants prosper.*

Selecting winners

BELOW *Variation is a facility that is common to all living things. Man however has shuffled the genetic pack of cards, coming up with an infinite number of varieties within the clematis genus. It takes many years of hard work to select a variety with appealing characteristics and then launch it on to the horticultural market, which is exactly what Brother Stefan has done in Poland, producing the delightful varieties pictured below.*

C. 'Black Madonna'

UNNAMED CLEMATIS

Selection for color, hardiness and resistance is what producing new clematis is all about. The finest make the grade and are released to the trade. Below are two of the hopefuls that may well be decorating gardens in the future.

C. '426–93' (left) and C. '526–95' (below left)
Known only by their trial numbers, these unnamed but beautiful cultivars await selection or deselection from the years of rigorous appraisal for hardiness, resistance and color. If they can survive the rigors of Warsaw winters, they have at least passed one cultivation test.

C. 'Kardynal Wyszyński'

C. 'Polish Spirit' A.G.M.

C. 'Siostra Faustyna Kowalska'

C. 'Danuta'

C. 'Kacper'

C. 'Warszawska Nike'

CLEMATIS BY COLOR

S O DIVERSE are the colors of clematis that they have been used in gardens as an artist might mix palettes of colors. With such a range of color and seasonal flowering of clematis, the genus is increasingly used for defining ultimate borders and satisfying color persuasions. In this chapter we explore the various groups of colors, from white and cream to purple, deep pink to lavender, bringing together clematis of similar hues. Candy-striped clematis and clematis with dark flowers and foliage are dealt with separately. There is a degree of subjectivity dusted with the usual variation of color that one expects from any clematis, but the selections may help to set the scene around which other plants can be accommodated.

C. *cirrhosa* var. *balearica* A.G.M.
ABOVE *This clematis is distinguished by its dark foliage, though it also has interesting, red-speckled, open bell flowers.*

C. 'Madame Julia Correvon' A.G.M.
LEFT *With its large, bright rose-red flowers and yellow stamens, this is a vivid and particularly attractive viticella type.*

Introduction to color

To accurately identify the colors of clematis can pose a real challenge. There are many variables to take into consideration and shades can change according to the time of year, the age of the clematis and where it is growing.

INTERPRETING COLOR in clematis is complex. There is a veritable feast of natural variation to consider, along with the facts that flowers change with time and according to the type of soil and the seasons. There is also the difficulty of capturing the right hue on photographic film as well as the trueness of printers' separations. If all these factors were to come together harmoniously, identification would be easy.

In this book, color has been considered for its own sake, on an individual basis, since gardeners simply enjoy clematis flowers for their color and often express their enthusiasms through color-coordinated borders. Garden designers make special places for particular shades of clematis. We have dealt with color in a logical manner, blending one color into the next (where possible). The majority of clematis figure in pinks and reds via purples and lavenders to blues. White to cream,

cream to yellow, dark forms and striped clematis are dealt with separately, since these belong to unnatural groups.

Reference points

There are various reference points for clematis color, but they are not always helpful. Britain's Royal Horticultural Society (R.H.S.) published a Color Fan in 1995, which is a standard reference work for horticulturalists but does not recognise the terms 'mauve', 'pink' or 'white' in its 808 color shades. Cultivars such as *C. montana* 'Pink Perfection' and *C.* 'Pink Pearl' are best left with descriptive cultivar names, while it is preferable to describe 'Mrs. Cholmondely' A.G.M. as blue rather than 'Violet 88C' as decreed by the R.H.S. Determining the right shade is impossible for many clematis. In some cases, color swatches supplied by paint firms are helpful.

Main color groups

The living world has never evolved to fit tidily into classification boxes, even when man's hand has influenced plant selection. Such is the case with clematis color. On the following pages, clematis have been gathered into 10 main color groups. Of course, there are always overlaps at the edges of our classification and the vagaries of biochemical content, age, individual variation and so on—all have a bearing on clematis color. The color groups are: THIS PAGE (CLOCKWISE FROM TOP LEFT) *White to cream; cream to yellow; pale to mid-pink; mid- to deep pink.* OPPOSITE PAGE (CLOCKWISE FROM TOP LEFT) *Deep pink to red; maroon to purple; purple; lilac to lavender; lavender to light blue; purple to deep blue.*

C. 'Belle of Woking'

C. cirrhosa 'Wisley Cream'

C. 'Hagley Hybrid'

C. 'Ruby Glow'

Color warning!
LEFT *Clematis colors change: in late spring to early summer, the sepals of C. 'Corona' are bright purple-pink. In late summer, however, the flowers are lighter in color.*

C. 'Crimson King'

C. 'Maureen'

C. 'Kacper'

C. 'Joan Picton'

C. 'Ulrique'

C. 'Beauty of Worcester'

White to cream

Creating a white clematis garden allows plenty of choice. Although a pure white clematis with white sepals and boss is hard to come by, there are about 20 varieties of white- to cream-sepaled clematis, all of which have their attractions.

MOST OF the favorite, white-sepaled clematis, such as 'Edith' A.G.M., 'The Bride' or 'Guernsey Cream', have yellow or cream centers. *C.* 'Pennell's Purity' is the whitest clematis around, although it looks more like a peony or double rose. *C. alpina* subsp. *sibirica* 'White Moth' has a pure white color and 'Belle of Woking' comes close but it can go a little green in the center, as with 'Duchess of Edinburgh'. *C.* 'Arctic Queen' and 'The Bride' would do well on any arbor with their pure white sepals and pale straw-colored centers. *En masse*, white clematis can look effective up a wall or over a garden gate,

as in *C.* 'Marie Boisselot' A.G.M. or *C.* 'John Huxtable'. For a 'white snow' effect caused by masses of flowers, *C. fargesii*, *C. recta* or *C. potaninii* would do the trick, although one has to accept a suffusion of cream into the whiteness.

Dotted around the white garden there are three white clematis that are good lookers, good flowerers, do well in containers and fade to pure white. It is a failing of many clematis that they fade to white, but it is done to perfection by 'Gillian Blades' A.G.M., 'Miss Bateman' A.G.M. and 'Snow Queen'—regarded by some as the finest of all whites. A new favorite is *C.* 'Jan Pawel II' (Pope John Paul II).

C. 'John Huxtable'
FAR LEFT *For a fine display in a white garden, the flower features of this plant make it quite distinctive.*

C. alpina subsp. sibirica 'White Moth'
LEFT *The fluffy nature of the flowers make this a delight to decorate any wall.*

C. 'Miss Bateman' A.G.M.
LEFT *A firm favorite, this plant has large, white sepals, contrasting red anthers and a compact, free-flowering habit in early summer.*

C. 'The Bride'
LEFT *This is one of the purest whites on the market.*

C. 'Paul Farges' (C. x *fargesioides* 'Summer Snow')
RIGHT *Small and delicate, the flowers have a large boss.*

C. 'Guernsey Cream'
RIGHT *From the Channel Islands, this plant has creamy white sepals and yellow anthers.*

C. 'Marie Boisselot' A.G.M.
LEFT *Vigorous and floriferous, this is a splendid plant beside a garden gate.*

C. 'Belle of Woking'
LEFT *With its pretty, double flowers and creamy white anthers, this is well worth having in the herbaceous border.*

C. 'Akemi'
RIGHT *The large, strident flowers are attractive in their uniform whiteness, including the male filaments, which are surmounted by cream anthers.*

C. 'Snow Queen'

This New Zealand hybrid was raised by Alister Keay and introduced to the gardening public by Jim Fisk in 1983. It is a compact plant, and free-flowering.

The large flowers of 'Snow Queen' are usually white, with a dash of pink (as here) or pale blue, especially in later blooms. The stamens are constant, being a striking, subdued red.

Cream to yellow

From pale creamy yellows to bright yellows to yellows with a hint of green, there are numerous varieties available that will bring a touch of sunshine to any corner of the garden.

A S A COLOR, yellow is impeccably addressed in a cultivar such as C. 'Golden Tiara', which has bright yellow sepals and chocolate-colored stamens. Yellow is subtly introduced with cream in such wild species as *C. ligusticifolia*, while creamy yellow verging on green is seen in *C. cirrhosa* 'Wisley Cream'.

The bell-shaped flowers of 'Wisley Cream' pale to insignificance beside the chunky yellow flowers of *C. grewiifolia*, a species clematis from the Himalayas with flower bells at least twice the size. Yellows and greens are very close, especially with the double *C. florida* 'Alba Plena' with its greenish centers. Green is taken to perfection with *C.* 'Alba Luxurians' A.G.M., which has green splashes on its sepals. Anyone wishing to create a yellow-themed garden could not go wrong with the vigorous vine *C. rehderiana* A.G.M. (see below). A suitable yellow hybrid for the front of the border might be 'Moonlight', which opens with a delicate hue of yellow with a touch of green, or with similarly colored *C.* 'Wada's Primrose'.

For an early showing, *C. cirrhosa* var. *balearica* A.G.M. has an unusual coloring, with yellow to the outside of the sepals and a splattering of purple-red marks on the inside. This is a vigorous plant that can become a tangle after a few years.

C. 'Moonlight'
ABOVE *Crisp in its yellowness with a touch of green, the flowers of this plant pale as it grows older.*

C. rehderiana A.G.M.
LEFT *Tiny bells borne in profusion make this a popular choice for all those who want good clematis cover.*

C. cirrhosa 'Wisley Cream'
BELOW *An evergreen plant with glossy, yellow-green leaves, the flowers are a delicate, dusty yellow and are bell-shaped.*

C. 'Golden Tiara'
LEFT *Large, yellow, bell-shaped flowers with a dark center typifies this variety. It is a vigorous and reliable performer.*

C. 'Wada's Primrose'
ABOVE *Soft yellow colors suffuse the sepals of this magnificent hybrid, a product of Japanese breeding.*

C. microphylla
LEFT *Small, star-like, yellow flowers cover this plant.*

C. 'Annamieke'
RIGHT *Small, star-like flowers with yellow sepals arise from soft green foliage.*

C. ligusticifolia

The Western virgin's bower is a species clematis that occurs as a native plant from Canada, through Montana, south to New Mexico in the United States. The name describes the privet shape of its leaves.

Like many European species, such as old man's beard, the flowers of C. ligusticifolia are small and numerous. The plant is vigorous and can become quite invasive once established in an area.

C. florida 'Alba Plena'
LEFT *A double white by Latin name, the sepals of this magnificent clematis do have a distinctive, green hue.*

Pale to mid-pink

There are a great many pink (and purple) clematis, many of which have been named after the fairer sex. The delicate hues of pink are absolutely outstanding—and a challenge to any rose.

THE SOFT, pale pink of montanas is always a welcome sight in spring. Among them there are a number of pale pink cultivars such as var. *rubens* A.G.M., 'Elizabeth' A.G.M. and the double 'Marjorie', which looks magnificent *en masse*. It is characteristic of montanas to be floriferous, and 'Continuity'—as its name implies—flowers over a long period. As an example of herbaceous clematis, *C.* x *jouiniana* 'Praecox' A.G.M. is good value with its two-tone, pink and white flowers often visited by butterflies. Verging toward purple, *C.* 'Minuet' A.G.M. can also make a big statement beside a porch, against a wall or up an arbor. If roses also happen to be your passion, *C.* 'Countess of Lovelace' with its balls of pale pink, double flowers is recommended. *C.* 'Hagley Hybrid' is a popular choice and a long-time flowerer. Its flowers are rich pink initially but fade to an agreeable, delicate shade of pink.

The subtle pink of 'Comtesse de Bouchaud' A.G.M. is very attractive, while one of the prettiest, daintiest and palest pink clematis is *C.* 'Little Nell', which has wavy, pink edges to its sepals and white inners. Larger hybrids of a pale pink persuasion include *C.* 'Rose Supreme', *C.* 'Madame Baron Veillard' and 'Caroline' or, a little darker and richer, 'Miss Crawshay'.

C. 'Rose Supreme'
LEFT *These large, pink sepals have a very delicate hue, contrasting with a suffusion of yellow over the boss.*

C. 'Edward Prichard'
LEFT *Perfect at the back of a herbaceous border, the star-like qualities of the upstanding flowers of this plant make it quite a spectacle when flowering en masse.*

C. macropetala 'Markham's Pink' A.G.M.
LEFT *Macropetalas are good value in the garden as their characteristic flowers provide a bright distraction in a range of pastel colors.*

C. 'Little Nell'
LEFT *Flicked back like a petticoat, the petals are not always this pink yet always have creamy centers.*

C. 'Charissima'
BELOW LEFT *Crowded together, the flowers are a collection of pinks, reds and white.*

C. 'Caroline'
LEFT *Delicate pink flowers make this an attractive variety with uniform-shaped sepals that are pinker along the bar.*

C. 'Hagley Hybrid'
LEFT *A great favorite, this is one of the most reliable and least demanding clematis on the market.*

C. 'Proteus'
ABOVE *Mauve-pink flowers are produced, which may be single, semi-double or double.*

C. 'Comtesse de Bouchaud' A.G.M.
ABOVE *This classic clematis bears bright mauve-pink, rounded flowers with cream anthers.*

C. montana 'Elizabeth' A.G.M.
LEFT *The pinkness is so good among the montanas that it deserves its A.G.M. status.*

Mid- to deep pink

*Sugar-pink, blushing rose, deep red wine and ruby-red colors are
all conjured up in this consideration of mid- to deep pink clematis, which can provide
a truly rich and rewarding display.*

AMONG THE pinks, *C. alpina* 'Ruby' has strong pink sepals and is a good performer, shinning up arbors with its prolific open bells that go well with apple or cherry flowers. This is not to be confused with the hybrid, *C.* 'Ruby Glow', which has lush pink sepals suffused with green.

There are other 'ruby' clematis, such as 'Ruby Anniversary' and 'Ruby Lady', which would provide a suitable corner of ruby plants. Before marching straight into the darkest and strongest of the pinks, we should mention the virtues of the pink viticellas and the tiny, star-shaped *C.* x *triternata* 'Rubromarginata' A.G.M., which can produce a snowy effect of pink and white in the herbaceous border at the height of summer.

Notable hybrids

Among the hybrids there is 'Hanaguruma' (see right), *C.* 'Asao' with its disproportionate central boss, to the regular *C.* 'Twilight'. From Poland, Brother Stefan introduced 'Danuta' (see below). *C.* 'Nikolai Rubstov', 'Margot Koster' and 'Voluceau' have firm flowers with strong colors and are recommended for borders and walls. A new cultivar, *C.* 'Kaarn', emphasises the blend of purple with dark pink.

C. 'Vino'
LEFT C. *'Vino's rich pink sepals are entirely uniform and add consistency to any border.*

C. 'Ruby Glow'
BELOW *Vibrant pink is well illustrated in this particular cultivar, which has wavy edges to its sepals.*

C. 'Danuta'
ABOVE *Polish* C. *'Danuta' has pronounced, central ridges along the sepals.*

C. viticella hybrid
LEFT *Masses of flowers are typical of this species.*

C. 'Asao'

LEFT *Opening in its finery, this hybrid has pointed sepals with slightly folded edges and a yellow boss.*

C. 'Jackmanii Rubra'

LEFT *The darkest pink by far, the petals of this clematis are matched only by its central boss of yellow stamens.*

C. 'Margot Koster'

LEFT *Tapered spatulas radiate out from the yellow center of this attractive cultivar.*

C. 'Princess of Wales'

LEFT *Upstanding, with tulip-like flowers, this texensis hybrid has deep pink to red flowers. As it grows older, the flowers open up even more.*

C. 'Colette Deville'

RIGHT *Showing the variation from dark pink to red, newly opened flowers are red while fully opened flowers are rich pink.*

C. 'Hanagurama'

LEFT *The name of this delightfully pink hybrid refers to the colorful "flower cars" seen in typical Japanese parades.*

C. alpina 'Ruby'

This hybrid is good value mixed with other plants, such as ornamental apples, where the white apple blossom picks out the white, central boss of the clematis.

Masses of pink flowers crowd together on a vigorous plant to produce a wonderful display. The pink bells open out with age and the plant can be grown at low level to medium height, supported in a border.

Deep pink to red

Although nature produces very few red clematis, there are a number of exciting, new hybrids that have been developed—certainly enough to liven up any herbaceous border or corner of a patio or deck.

REDS IN clematis in nature are quite rare, but are typical of the North American species clematis *C. texensis*. This species has therefore been the source of some of the redness seen in some of the red clematis known today: For example, *C.* 'The Princess of Wales' or *C.* 'Sir Trevor Lawrence'.

Ecclesiastical reds are remembered in *C.* 'Rouge Cardinal' and *C.* 'Kardynal Wyszyński' raised by Brother Stefan in Poland and introduced by Jim Fisk in Suffolk, England in 1986. Also introduced by Jim Fisk, but in 1984, is 'Allanah', which was raised by Alister Keay in New Zealand.

C. 'Crimson King' is a very uniform, red-magenta color with a central boss of cream, making it very distinctive. Two fiery-looking clematis, which go by the names of *C.* 'Firefly' and *C.* 'Fireworks' A.G.M., have reds of slightly different shades—'Fireworks' having a two-tone arrangement of color along the axis of each sepal.

Large-flowered hybrids

Other large-flowered hybrids that have red flowers are *C.* 'Akaishi', 'Doctor Ruppel' A.G.M. and 'Myôjô'. 'Myôjô' makes a good subject for a container. *C.* 'Kommerei' is a super, red clematis, which has red-tipped stamens as well as uniform red sepals. This is a new cultivar from Germany. *C.* 'Pôhjanael' is of viticella origin and also has uniform red sepals.

From the same stock, *C.* 'Abundance' is red, too. A favorite to go rambling through roses is 'Ville de Lyon', which in certain lights has a silvery tinge or whitish dusting to the sepals, giving it a unique characteristic. A new hybrid, *C.* 'Rüütel', is a dark and very rich red.

C. 'Fireworks' A.G.M.

A great bonus to any garden from spring to autumn, this successful and vigorous cultivar was raised by John Treasure of Burford House Gardens in the early 1980s.

The free-flowering 'Fireworks' boasts large, mauve-purple flowers with petunia-red bars and dark red anthers. Its wavy sepals and strident coloring give this clematis a great deal of presence.

C. 'Akaishi'
LEFT *Slightly different in its hue of colors to 'Fireworks', this cultivar is equally striking.*

C. 'Etoile Rose'
LEFT *Numerous, rosy red flowers are highly typical —they open out with age.*

C. 'Kardynal Wyszyński'
LEFT *Cardinal-red flowers, fit for this Polish cardinal, are exhibited by these bright flowers.*

C. 'Crimson King'
ABOVE *Known as 'Crimson Star' in America, the bright crimson flowers surround a yellow boss and may be single or semi-double.*

C. 'Madame Julia Correvon' A.G.M.
ABOVE *This viticella cultivar has four to five well-separated sepals that are arching and curved.*

C. 'Allanah'
ABOVE *Black anthers and deep red sepals are characteristic of this compact cultivar, which was bred in New Zealand.*

C. 'Ville de Lyon'
ABOVE *Raised in France in 1899, this has wide but tapered sepals whose color can change according to the luster of the leaf.*

C. 'Sir Trevor Lawrence'
LEFT *Red sepals denote this cultivar, whose flowers open out from their original, tulip shape.*

C. 'Rüütel'
ABOVE *The red sepals are wide and simply shaped, enclosing a dark boss.*

Maroon to purple

Maroon colors are tricky to place, coming midway between reds and purples, but they represent the amazing, velvety look that many of these examples exhibit—the kind of rich colors that make you want to stroke their sepals.

BECAUSE THERE is no precise maroon boundary, the clematis on these pages range from purple-reds to burgundy-reds. Suffice it to say that the word 'velours', as in *C.* 'Royal Velours' A.G.M., is the French word for velvet and also describes the characteristic plush or velvet texture. The 'Royal' is hardly surprising, since purples have traditionally been associated with royalty since earliest times. It crops up again as *C.* 'Royalty' A.G.M., which has a combination of a central, red spar and purple outers to its sepals. It is remarkable that a flower as simple as clematis can produce such an immaculate spectacle.

C. 'Niobe' A.G.M., *C.* 'Gizela' and *C.* 'Stazik' are perfectionists at the velvet approach. These three clematis have central European origins, since 'Niobe' A.G.M. was raised by Wladyslaw Noll in Poland (and introduced by Jim Fisk in 1975). 'Gizela' (after the Queen of Hungary in the 10th century) is a more recent hybrid from Germany and 'Stazik' comes from the Baltic states. *C.* 'Maureen' is a purer purple-red with overtones of 'Royalty' colors and patterns.

No fewer than five A.G.M. plants figure on these pages for their velvety attractions. Adding a bit of blue to the maroon, there is *C.* 'Abundance', which is a viticella type. Going to the reds, another viticella, 'Tango', has deep red sepals. *C.* 'Star of India' A.G.M. makes a fine display with its symmetrical, star-like effect of purple-red and pointed sepals. The jackmanii are perfectionists at deep purple-reds and *C.* 'Jackmanii Superba' and its relative '*C.* 'Serenata' are good examples from this indulgent color selection.

C. 'Stazik'

The velvety texture of the sepals looks amazingly real in this cultivar, which has full and slightly overlapping sepals. It also has a tendency to produce semi-double features.

The center of each sepal is rich, dark red and, on the edges, a velvety brown, which in some lights has a distinct, purple sheen. The dark color is continued into the anthers, which are tipped in chocolate.

C. 'Romantika'
ABOVE *This has flowers that are slightly lighter purple than its jackmanii parent.*

C. 'Abundance'
LEFT *Purple sepals that taper at the base are typical of this clematis.*

C. 'Gipsy Queen' A.G.M.
LEFT *Rich, velvety purple flowers make this a sought-after A.G.M. plant.*

C. 'Royal Velours' A.G.M.
LEFT *Deserving of its A.G.M. mark, this dark, velvety clematis has relatively small flowers, the sepals of which are rounded with reflexed tips. The dark center, replete with green filaments and black anthers, is most dramatic. 'Royal Velours' was introduced to the U.K. by William Robinson and his gardener, Ernest Markham, earlier this century. Growing to about 10ft. (3m.), it is best shown off against light-colored foliage, such as salix or ceanothus.*

C. 'Star of India' A.G.M.
LEFT *Star-like in form, with four to six radiating sepals each ending in a fine tip, this is a striking clematis with dark purple bars.*

C. 'Royalty' A.G.M.
LEFT *Royal families have long been associated with the prestigious color of purple, which was once very difficult to acquire. This clematis has semi-double flowers early on.*

C. 'Gizela'
ABOVE *A promising cultivar, this has an accentuated, cream boss and dark purple sepals.*

C. 'Niobe' A.G.M.
ABOVE *Like 'Gizela' in color and form, but with more uniform features, this specimen has a large boss.*

C. 'Maureen'
ABOVE *Red to maroon colors are mixed to good effect in this large-sepaled cultivar.*

Purple

Purple is often the color associated with clematis, especially the purple of the jackmanii hybrids, which excel as relatively vigorous vines up walls or over arbors, porches and arches.

NONE OF the clematis on these pages is species clematis, for there is little in the way of native purple clematis. Most of the rich purples are singles, but as well as jackmanii, which can be semi-double or double, there is also C. 'Vyvyan Pennell' A.G.M., which can have tightly formed flowers.

C. 'The President' A.G.M. is a popular, reliable and long-flowering clematis that has been around since 1876 when it was raised by nurseryman Charles Noble of Sunningdale, England. The curvaceous lines of a fresh C. 'Elsa Späth' A.G.M. accentuate the deep purple-blue sepals and its attractive, red stamens. This was also raised in Germany, in 1891, and it too flowers for a long time. Of more recent origin, C. 'Haku-Ôkan' (see below) was first introduced by Jim Fisk in 1971. A late-flowering, long-flowering delight for arches and doorways is C. 'Petit Faucon'. This was raised by Raymond Evison in 1989 from a chance seedling of C. 'Daniel Deronda' A.G.M. Its sepals could not be smaller and more 'petite' and totally diminished in relation to its anthers.

On a much larger scale, C. 'Marie Louise Jensen' is strikingly magnificent for the same reason: the sepals are very small in relation to its superb boss of pink-tipped, white anthers. The firmness of the flowers make this Swedish introduction quite delectable. There are many more purple clematis than can be shown on these pages, such as 'Lasurstern', 'Pietr Skarga', 'Madame Edouard André' and 'Nuit de Chine'.

C. 'Centre Attraction'
LEFT *Relatively small, purple flowers with a bright yellow center make this an attractive clematis.*

C. 'Burma Star'
ABOVE *Strident in its purple colors, the sepals are pointed to give 'Burma Star' a cartwheel effect.*

C. 'Haku-Ôkan'
ABOVE *'Haku-Ôkan', or 'White Royal Crown', is not very vigorous, even in the ground, but its rich colors, darker when young, make up for any lack of performance.*

C. 'The President' A.G.M.
FAR LEFT *The large, wavy sepals are deep purple.*

C. 'Petit Faucon'
ABOVE LEFT *The large boss supports twisted, purple sepals.*

C. 'Duchess of Sutherland'
LEFT *Usually soft magenta in color, this specimen is reddish purple.*

C. 'Kacper'
LEFT *Large, purple sepals have prominent, dark purple bars.*

C. 'Vyvyan Pennell' A.G.M.
RIGHT *Double purple is exhibited in a two-tone color scheme.*

C. 'Marie Louise Jensen'
FAR LEFT *This has bright purple flowers and spiky sepals.*

C. 'Hagley Hybrid' A.G.M.
LEFT *With rather pointed sepals and dark-tipped stamens, this hybrid is a soft purple.*

Lilac to lavender

There are an enormous number of lavenders among clematis, many of which are named after women, like the pinks. Lavender has touches of red and blue, reflecting the great range of shades in this group.

AMONG THE double lavenders, C. 'Denny's Double' and 'Countess of Lovelace' are both worthy of mention. More of a double pink-lavender is C. 'John Gould Veitch', whose flower is not so divided.

The Raymond Evison introduction of 1997, C. 'Blue Moon', is of the palest lavender, making its crinkly sepal edges particularly attractive. Its color makes it look almost ethereal and, as the name aptly suggests, it reminds one of pale, gleaming moonlight.

Jim Fisk of Suffolk, England named his new hybrid with its wisteria-blue colors C. 'Alice Fisk', after his wife, in 1967. C. 'Barbara Jackman' was raised by the Jackmans in 1952 and has lavender sepals with a darker, sometimes reddish bar and contrasting, yellow anthers. Flowering from late spring to early summer, its blooms tend to fade in strong sun. Some clematis within this colour range flower both on last year's growth as well as current growth, which is a fairly rare phenomenon in clematis. Among these are the very vigorous C. 'Lilacina Floribunda', which was raised by Cripps and Sons in England in 1880, and C. 'Perrin's Pride', raised by Steffen Clematis Nursery in New York State, America, and introduced to Europe by Evison in the 1980s.

C. 'Proteus' is a vigorous clematis that produces large, double, semi-double and, later in the season, single flowers. Its sepals are suffused with yellow and green, making it an unusual and distinctive plant. C. 'Belle Nantaise', raised by Boisselot in France in 1887, has large lavender blue to violet-purple flowers up to 8in. (20cm.) in diameter and prominent yellow anthers.

C. 'Barbara Jackman'
TOP LEFT *The smooth-edged lavender sepals of this plant are distinctive, especially with the dark bar in the center.*

C. 'Lilacina Floribunda'
TOP RIGHT *This is appropriately named after its numerous, lilac flowers.*

C. 'King Edward VII'
BOTTOM LEFT *Pale lavender-lilac is typical here, with a pale boss.*

C. 'Alice Fisk'
BOTTOM RIGHT *Lilac-mauve sepals makes this a very special clematis.*

C. 'Proteus'
LEFT *Blossoming to its full double lavender with green and yellow suffusion, this is a truly magnificent variety.*

C. 'Joan Picton'
RIGHT *Pink-lilac sepals encircle red- tipped stamens on this attractive plant.*

C. 'Blue Moon'
LEFT *More lilac than blue, this is an impressive, new clematis introduced to the trade in 1997 by Raymond Evison.*

C. 'Beata'
ABOVE *Strong lilac flowers with purple centers are typical of this variety.*

C. 'Belle Nantaise'
LEFT *This plant is very variable—even as it grows it produces lavender and purple-violet flowers on the same plant.*

C. 'Roko Kolla'
ABOVE *Subtlety in hue makes this a remarkable variety with its curvaceous and slightly wavy sepals.*

Lavender to light blue

*It is difficult to find any other plants in the living world that can
compete with the variety of shades offered by clematis in what is one of their specialist colors.
The clematis on these pages offer a mere glimpse of the subtle hues on offer.*

THERE IS a texture to many clematis which gives the impression that the sepals are made from delicate crushed silk, calico, velvet or even ruffled paper. Such is the exquisite structure of the plant that it is difficult to tell the difference.

The lavender to light blues illustrated here range from the medium sized to the largest clematis of all, which are magnificent in their fine colors. Capturing the right hue on film, catching the cultivar on its best day and fitting these masterpieces from the clematis genus into the jigsaw of matching colors is not only tricky but also subjective, since there are many other contenders for this color group.

There are a couple of lavender to light blue clematis with women's names, such as *C.* 'Laura', which has large, rounded sepals, and another

hybrid *C.* 'Ulrique', which has wavy edges to its sepals. Both have dark centers. Another lavender flower with a slightly pinkish hue is *C.* 'Vanessa', which recalls the colors of montanas. It was raised by Vince and Sylvia Denny of Preston, England in 1995 and is a cross between 'Sylvia Denny' and 'Perle d'Azur' A.G.M.

It was in 1952 that the large blue dinner plates of *C.* 'Fuji-musume' were introduced from Japan. This clematis has large, floppy sepals and makes a big splash of color in the garden. *C.* 'Ivan Olsson' displays particularly unusual colouring, its lavender to pale blue sepals having a broad, creamy white central bar. The flower fades prettily to a shade of ice blue and its red anthers strike a dramatic contrast. *C.* 'Special Occasions' is a seedling from 'Mrs Cholomondely' which has wide pale blue flowers and is ideal for a container.

C. 'Queen Alexandra'
LEFT *Raised by the Jackmans of Woking, England, this has lavender flowers and will grow to about 10ft. (3m.). It has wavy sepal edges and a yellow boss.*

C. 'Denny's Double'
LEFT *Raised by Vince and Sylvia Denny, the flowers are produced in late spring and again in early autumn. It can be grown in sun or shade.*

C. 'Rosalie'
Raised in Warsaw, Poland, by Brother Stefan and introduced in 1997, this pretty, pinkish lavender cultivar produces flowers from late spring to late summer.

The wide and pointed sepals of C. 'Rosalie' have slightly wavy edges and the anthers are yellow.

C. 'Signe'
LEFT *The flowers are large and flamboyant with attractive, wavy edges to the sepals, which have a faint, rosy bar.*

C. 'Vanessa'
RIGHT *Raised by the Dennys of Preston, England in 1995, this has 'Sandra Denny' and 'Perle d'Azur' A.G.M. as parents.*

C. 'Special Occasions'
LEFT *Raised by Ken Pyne in 1995, this has recurved sepals with a hint of green at the base and blooms in mid-summer.*

C. 'Fuji-musume'
LEFT *Large and beautiful, this possesses the genes of 'The President' A.G.M. and was raised by Sejuru Arai in 1952.*

C. 'Laura'
ABOVE *This has large, floppy sepals with maroon-chocolate anthers and yellow filaments, making it a very attractive clematis.*

C. 'Ivan Olsson'
ABOVE *A seedling of 'The President' A.G.M., this was raised by Magnus Johnson in Sweden in 1955 and can be grown in any aspect. The color of this specimen is somewhat faded.*

C. 'Ulrique'
ABOVE *Bright in color, the sepals are crenulated with a prominent bar and the anthers are velvety maroon, supported on white filaments.*

Purple to deep blue

Purple is the signature color of many a fine clematis, but here we look at a few that begin to venture into the realms of blue. Variety of shape and vigor are still prominent.

THERE WAS a spate of deep blue clematis raised at the end of the 19th century, among them one of the earliest deep blue-purples, C. 'Jackmanii Superba', developed between 1870 and 1890 by the Jackmans. It has fuller sepals than the ordinary C. 'Jackmanii' A.G.M. They later went on to raise the periwinkle-blue C. 'Mrs. P.B. Truax'. Another deep blue clematis is C. 'Daniel Deronda' A.G.M., created by Charles Noble in 1992. This has large semi-double or single flowers in early summer, followed by smaller, single flowers, with creamy yellow anthers.

C. 'Beauty of Worcester', raised in 1886 in Worcester, England by Richard Smith & Co., has deep blue double flowers in early summer, followed by single flowers (see opposite). C. 'H.F. Young' A.G.M., raised in 1962, was regarded as one of the best blue clematis on the market until recently. Since then C. 'Europa', 'Jenny' and 'Frau Mikiko' have been produced in Germany, and in Poland Brother Stefan is developing the deep blue C. '239–89'. From Holland, C. 'Multi Blue' is a unique sport of 'The President' A.G.M., which has a bizarre structure of two sets of sepals—outer ones that look like most clematis and a whirl of tiny inner ones, giving it a double, "multi" status. The outer sepals fall to leave an even more unusual clematis. From Sweden in 1960 came C. 'Serenata' introduced by Tage Lundell, which flowers from late summer.

C. 'Lord Nevill' A.G.M.
FAR LEFT *One of the darkest blues available, this has tinges of purple and slightly wavy sepals. The boss is lighter.*

C. X cylindrica
LEFT *A useful low, sprawling hybrid, this has nodding bells of blue-purple.*

C. 'Frau Mikiko'
LEFT *The large sepals of a purple-blue hue are very slightly wavy.*

C. 'Multi Blue'
LEFT *Some flowers lose their outer sepals and produce a boss-like center of sepals in this very characteristic fashion.*

C. 'Mrs. P.B. Truax'
BELOW *Violet-blue to purple, the flowers are borne prolifically on this plant.*

C. 'Europa'
ABOVE *Large, uniform-sized sepals of a purple hue set off the yellowish center of this fine flower.*

C. 'Jenny'
LEFT *The four sepals are quite separate and reflexed, and the boss is pale yellow.*

C. 'Beauty of Worcester'
ABOVE *Large flowers with pointed, purple-blue sepals can decorate any arbor with great ease.*

Dark foliage and flowers

For those seeking to explore the darker side of clematis, there are several very distinctive forms of foliage, particularly among the montanas, as well as some beautifully dusky flowers.

THE TWO staples for dark foliage are the montanas and *C. recta* 'Purpurea'. Many of the montanas generously produce dark bronzy, new growth, which can look very attractive. The foliage is a little shiny with a touch of red. They then settle down to more muted greens as the shoots mature.

C. montana 'Freda' A.G.M. is especially attractive with its dark leaflets and pink flowers. *C.m.* 'Warwickshire Rose' has tiny, eye-like flowers set in a sea of uniform, dark brown leaves. *C.m.* 'Broughton Star's leaves are red-brown and produced in large quantities, like those of *C.m.* 'Alexander' and for foliage alone are valuable over a trellis or on a wall. The herbaceous perennial *C. recta* includes a form called 'Purpurea', which has rich chocolate brown-colored, upright stems and leaves that contrast distinctly with its white flowers. This is widely available and makes an invaluable contribution in the middle of a herbaceous border when growing through other plants.

If you are spoiled for choice of dark foliage among the montanas, there are also some dark and dusky clematis flowers worth considering to explore this darker side of clematis. There is a species clematis, *C. fusca*, native to east Asia that has small, dark flowers—"fusca" meaning dark in Latin. *C. orientalis* 'Red Balloon' has attractive, dusky-red, orange peel-like flowers held high above its pale green leaflets. This is a new introduction from Germany.

C. 'La Daciana' has much smaller flowers, which are reflexed and the upperside is marked with dark reddish speckles.

C. recta 'Purpurea'
ABOVE *In this specimen, the darkness of the leaves and stems is intense and well worth having, because it highlights the pale flowers. In some clones, the purple hue is very insipid.*

C. montana 'Freda' A.G.M.
LEFT *A reliable montana to have about the purple border, the pink flowers contrast well with the dark foliage.*

C. tibetana subsp. vernayi A.G.M.
LEFT *Dusted in dark speckles, the reflexed sepals enclose dark stamens.*

C. montana 'Broughton Star'

FAR LEFT *Doubleness in small-sized clematis can look stunning close up.*

C. montana 'Warwickshire Rose'

ABOVE LEFT *The rich pinkness of the tiny flowers is picked up in the leaflet stems.*

C. 'Negritjanka'

LEFT *Superb symmetry is seen here in the dark sepals, which are perfectly tapered.*

C. campaniflora 'Lisboa'

ABOVE *A dark version of the normal, white flowers gives added attraction, especially to the reflexed nature of the sepals.*

C. 'Red Balloon'

LEFT *Yellow and ocher are well combined in these orange peel-type flowers that will decorate any fence or trelliswork.*

Candy-striped clematis

Striping in clematis is not unusual but some do it more than others. Striping is aligned along the length of the sepal and in some hybrids it is so characteristic that it is used as an identification feature.

STRIPING IS always aligned along the length of the sepal, centered along the mid-line bars (if present), either on the upper or lower side. It is often used as an identification feature—the best example being C. 'Huldine', which has pink-tinged stripes on the underside of its white sepals. A hybrid from Germany, C. 'Entel' boasts similar underside markings. C. 'Twilight' has an unusual color combination of pale yellow and pink only on the underside, and is particularly effective when seen in evening light, which seems to accentuate it.

Striping often creates a star-like appearance and sometimes (but not always) this is reflected in the name of the clematis. One of the best-known, striped clematis, with a star-like appearance, is

C. 'Nelly Moser' A.G.M., raised by Moser in 1897 (see box). A stronger-colored clematis, 'Sugar Candy' makes quite a spectacle with its wheel of light and dark pink sepals. Another impressive, striped clematis is C. 'Venosa Violacea' A.G.M. Two-tone, striped shades are also found in such clematis as the viticella 'Elvan' with centers that are lighter than the outers.

It is exceedingly common in clematis to have a central, red bar along the top of the sepals, and this added touch can confer a high degree of distinctiveness and attractiveness to the flowers. Pronounced examples are C. 'Maureen', 'Mrs. N. Thompson' and 'Susan Allsop', while more subtle ones are C. 'Corona', 'Morning Cloud' (formerly 'Satsukibore') and 'Victoria'.

C. 'Huldine'
LEFT *Highly typical with its underside patterning, the striping is very obvious but not replicated on the top surface.*

C. 'Entel'
LEFT *Two pink, stripy ribs radiate across the pale pink sepals of this small-flowered hybrid.*

C. 'Nelly Moser' A.G.M.

This classic was originally raised in France in 1897 by Moser and went on to be awarded the prestigious A.G.M. for its particularly good, all-round performance. It grows to a few yards and produces lots of flowers in spring and summer.

Dark stripes run along the center line of each sepal, giving it a distinctive appearance. The effect of lots of blooms on a mature specimen is very striking and individual blooms can be cut for display. The large seed heads are also worth having.

C. 'Sugar Candy'
LEFT *The stripes on this large-flowered hybrid are so well-pronounced that it looks just like a cartwheel.*

C. 'Minuet' A.G.M.
LEFT *Tiny, viticella-like flowers are crossed by white bars radiating from the base of each sepal.*

C. 'Mrs. N. Thompson'
ABOVE *Wide, bluish-purple flowers with a dark red band running up the center line of each sepal are very attractive. A compact plant, this is ideal for small gardens or for growing in containers.*

C. 'Twilight'
LEFT *Cut and displayed especially to show the underside, the green-yellow stripes are in complete contrast to the rose-pink, upper surfaces.*

C. 'Venosa Violacea' A.G.M.
LEFT *Dramatic in the extreme, this false clone has been selected to make the most of contrasting purple-violet and white.*

C. 'Sakuramusum'
ABOVE *A white clematis with pink bars, or a pink clematis with white edges, this flower has extremely wide bars that take up most of the sepal.*

CLEMATIS FOR THE PLACE

CLEMATIS CAN be grown just about anywhere. They will shin up trees or unsightly tree stumps. They thrive as herbaceous plants (the herbaceous ones, that is) in borders where they will die down for the winter, and they do well at the back of the border climbing up walls and trellises. Within the border they race up frames and wind themselves around other border plants. They can grow beyond the bounds of the border and go wild over a patio or pathway in colorful fashion. They even flourish in containers and hanging baskets and can be grown up tripods like sweet peas. Provided they receive water, light and a little care and attention, clematis will reward the gardener with eye-catching displays, whatever the situation.

Climbing a pergola
ABOVE *Splashes of clematis color add to the vertical dimensions of a rustic pergola.*

C. 'Minuet' A.G.M.
LEFT *Smothering a wall with its masses of flowers, this is typical of viticellas.*

Walls

*Given half a chance, clematis will shin up walls and quickly cover them,
sometimes even smothering other plants in their claim for light and space. They have the great
advantage over ivies of not pulling out mortar or splitting bricks as they go.*

A S CLIMBERS or vines, clematis are expert at getting about when the season arrives, by means of twining leaves or stems or by using other plants for support. The typical English-style garden often has a decent-sized brick wall, which can be used with great aplomb to display clematis at the back of the tiered herbaceous border.

If you are planting clematis along a wall, allow at least 6ft. (2m.) separation between plants and secure the clematis with eyes. It is best to grow clematis alongside herbaceous plants and shrubs as this helps to avoid the legginess of some types, which produce masses of dead-looking stems with a bundle of flowers on top. The skill is to interweave the plants so that the flush of flowers emanates from an unexpected place, or to have two or three bushy clematis growing as a big mass together.

Clematis on walls can produce a wonderful display in just a few weeks from spring to summer.

Most of the deciduous ones die back to the ground during the winter and gallop upward to produce flowers in profusion by the spring. Early-flowering clematis, such as alpinas and macropetalas, should be planted in shadier, less exposed areas. Evergreen clematis, such as *C. armandii* or *C. cirrhosa* 'Wisley Cream', provide interest during the dormant months. Protection from prevailing winds and strong sunlight is best reserved for mauve and pink clematis, which tend to fade and under-perform in the sun. Clematis such as *C.* 'Ville de Lyon', *C.* 'Ernest Markham' A.G.M. and most blues and purples enjoy full sun, provided their roots are shaded. On walls that do not always have the sun, the alpina, montana and macropetala cultivars will all do well, as will hybrids such as 'Bees' Jubilee' A.G.M., 'Hagley Hybrid' 'Henryi' A.G.M., 'Jackmanii' A.G.M., 'Ken Donson' A.G.M., 'Nelly Moser' A.G.M., 'Scartho Gem' and 'William Kennett'.

C. 'Perle d'Azur' A.G.M.
LEFT *Shady walls are worth covering with this hybrid from jackmanii.*

C. 'Mrs. George Jackman' A.G.M.
BELOW LEFT *Flowering well on walls, this is a compact plant with lots of blooms.*

C. 'Nelly Moser' A.G.M.
RIGHT *A firm favorite and reliable flowerer, the only drawback of this plant is that its flowers fade.*

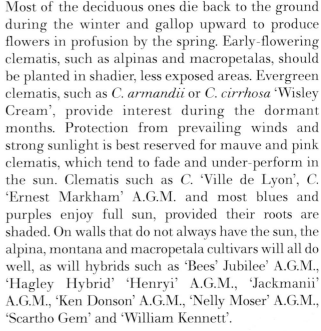

C. montana
LEFT *In typical fashion, this montana makes for a grand entrance into a walled garden.*

C. 'Twilight'
ABOVE *Try to grow clematis through other wall vegetation to avoid the lower, dead-looking stems from being too visible.*

A hedge of C. montana
LEFT *The pink, star-like flowers of this montana have formed an interesting matrix in this hedge.*

C. 'Countess of Lovelace' with roses
ABOVE *The pretty, pastel colorings of these clematis and climbing rose flowers are a picture on any wall.*

C. montana var. rubens A.G.M.
RIGHT *Hugging the wall in a wonderful display of springtime color, this cultivar is a great foil for the wall behind.*

Pillars and posts

Pillars covered with clematis are static displays that are worth a great deal in design terms within the garden. Overall, they add an extra vertical dimension to the garden and provide the gardener with some new challenges.

THE VERTICAL element in a garden is vigorously explored by clematis. Given the right structure, they are natural performers, creating perfect pillars of color. The obvious examples are old tree stumps: where a tree has to be felled or pollarded (cut off a few feet from the ground), the remaining stump is an ideal starting point for a pillar. Alternatively, a length of tree trunk about 10ft. (3m.) long can be sunk into the ground. Other pillars, obelisks or tripods can be made, or bought, and placed strategically in the garden to produce fabulous displays of clematis for all to see.

Montanas are the specialists at smothering pillars, and the best results are often achieved by varying the colors and planting two contrasting hybrids together, perhaps *C. montana* and *C.m.* 'Tetrarose' A.G.M.. A single clematis flowering up a single pole is far less interesting than if it were part of some other garden structure, such as the end of an arbor, fence or wall. Small pillars may be eye-catching in very small gardens, perhaps in a rural cottage-type garden, but a more distinctive approach to vertical gardening entails a variety of color and leaf form diffused laterally from the pillar. *C. montana* 'Freda' A.G.M. is a little more rampant than other montanas and has dark foliage that contrasts with its pink flowers. Another vigorous clematis, with the capacity to grow into trees, is *C.* 'Paul Farges'.

There are two aspects of clematis gardening not much practiced since William Robinson gardened at Gravetye Manor and wrote 'The Virgin's Bower' in 1912. The first is growing clematis up tripods or stakes, as one would do with sweet peas or scarlet runners; the second is growing clematis—montanas especially—as garlands to festoon outbuildings. There appears to be a lack of experimentation today compared with earlier in the 20th century, when many clematis were new to horticulture.

C. montana

LEFT *A typical pillar formed by a mature clematis, there is little room for vegetative growth. The tree stump could rot and collapse and the montana would remain unabashed.*

C. 'Madame Julia Correvon' A.G.M.

LEFT *Creating a fine display, this clematis enjoys the climb up a pillar and thrives in a sunny position.*

C. montana var. rubens A.G.M.

RIGHT *Montanas are best at this kind of coverage and, with careful training, can make a truly masterful display.*

Containers

There are many clematis that are eminently suited to pots, containers and even hanging baskets. Stone or plastic Versailles tubs or corner containers are ideal—whichever you choose, make sure that it is as large as possible.

THERE ARE well over 50 types of clematis suitable for containers, so everyone will have their own favorites. Up to three clematis can be planted in a single tub, although it is a bit of a squeeze and, since vigor and performance tend to decline in the third year in a pot, they will need to be replaced with other hybrids. Feeding with tomato fertiliser or slow-release pellets helps somewhat to overcome this.

The alpinas and macropetalas are good in pots and their fine foliage and flowers can be allowed to spill over. Other recommendations might include the reds, such as 'Bees' Jubilee' A.G.M., 'Carnaby' and 'Akaishi'; the blues, such as 'Multi Blue'; or the whites, such as 'Snow Queen' or *C. florida* 'Alba Plena'. Then there are the Japanese-named varieties such as 'Fuji-musume', 'Hikarugenji' and 'Kasugayama'. Probably my best performers in containers among the hybrids are *C.* 'Mrs. Cholmondeley' A.G.M., 'Wada's Primrose' and *C.* 'Hagley Hybrid', while my worst is undoubtedly *C.*

'Ladybird Johnson', which never achieves flowers because of its recurring wilt problem. For hanging baskets, choose hybrids or species that are not very vigorous by nature, such as the species clematis *C. forsteri* or a dwarf form of *C. tangutica*.

The advantage of gardening with containers is that they are movable and can be filled with your preferred color variety one season and replenished the next to meet new foliage or color designs. A disadvantage is that death through water starvation can occur in a day, so always water well and regularly. Another problem is waterlogging, which can occur when drainage holes get blocked. Mulching the top of the container can reduce water loss and keep the roots of the clematis cool.

Cultivating clematis in pots can be done very successfully, even on tiny balconies. As far as record-breakers go, it is possible to get a *C.* 'John Warren' with 150 flowers from a 12in. (30cm.) pot, and a *C.* 'Niobe' A.G.M. with 100 flowers from a similar container. Who needs *terra firma*?

C. 'Myôjô'
ABOVE *Ideal for a deck, the large, single flowers are always striking, but the plant needs fertilising to produce reliable blooms.*

C. flammula
LEFT *A foaming waterfall of flowers, the pure white clematis is eminently displayed in this 19th century* jardinière.

C. forsteri
LEFT *Growing in a small container, the tiny flowers and dark foliage are very attractive.*

C. 'Wada's Primrose'
RIGHT *Excellent at first in a container, its vigor and primrose color can be lost after a while, so it is best planted out in the garden after a couple of years.*

C. 'Mrs. Cholmondeley' A.G.M.
ABOVE *This is the autumn flush of flowers, which are smaller and lacking in the deep lavender blue of those in mid-summer, but no less unwelcome on any deck.*

C. macropetala
RIGHT *Stumped for more space, this atrogene has produced enough flowers to cover its static host.*

Clematis with roses

Roses and clematis are natural partners because the rose provides the firm basis through which clematis can climb or find some support. Mid-summer clematis are best grown with roses and in secluded corners you could choose scented plants for extra effect.

CLEMATIS AND roses are obvious partners, though the former can easily dominate the latter. Clematis need the support of something relatively rigid, and are rewarded doubly if that sturdy shrub is a climber. In the wild, the wild rose (*Rosa canina*) and *Clematis alpina* A.G.M. no doubt intermingle, the delicate shoots of the clematis being strewn about the care-free stems of the rose and producing a mixture of light blue, white and pink hues and green foliage.

In the garden the colors are contrived but effective, like the bold colors of *C.* 'Jackmanii' A.G.M. among the yellow-green of *Rosa rugosa* (see below). Gertrude Jekyll used to grow "a solid, continuously intermingling mass" of *Rosa* 'Madame Alfred Carrière' (now an A.G.M. plant) and *Clematis montana* on "stout larch posts" in her garden, providing a white and pink mélange of color (she does not state which montana). In my own garden I grow *C.* 'Stazik' with *Rosa* 'Masquerade' (both slow developers), *C.* 'Comtesse de Bouchaud' A.G.M. with *Rosa* 'Pink Perpètué', *C.* 'Ville de Lyon' with *Rosa* 'The Wife of Bath' and *C.* 'Etoile Violette' A.G.M. with *Rosa* 'Excelsa'. These are simply happy coincidences of color. *C.* 'Etoile Violette' A.G.M. also goes well with the damask moss rose *Rosa* 'William Lobb' A.G.M., a scented rose for mid-summer.

C. 'Stazik' with *Rosa* 'Masquerade'.
ABOVE *A reticent grower in the author's garden, 'Stazik' nevertheless comes together with the two-tone rose to create this effective color combination.*

C. 'Jackmanii' A.G.M. with *Rosa rugosa*
LEFT *A prolific grower, 'Jackmanii' will easily outstrip this rose but, while growing among it, can make a very pleasant diversion.*

Clematis and rose arbor
ABOVE *In a tranquil enclave in the garden, clematis and roses have been grown to form a delightful, scented arbor.*

C. **'Perle d'Azur' and** *Rosa* **'Morning Jewel'**
LEFT *This is an attractive, rose-clematis partnership in which the pinks and purples complement one another very well. C. 'Perle d'Azur' has mauve-purple sepals with a yellow boss.*

C. viticella **'Etoile Violette' A.G.M. with** *Rosa* **'William Lobb' A.G.M.**
LEFT *Close color coordination is achieved in this respectable marriage between two complementary partners.*

C. **'Ville de Lyon',** *Buddleia alternifolia* **A.G.M. and** *Rosa* **'Pink Favorite'**
RIGHT *Clematis, buddleia and roses make an exciting, triple combination.*

Clematis with other plants

Clematis combinations can either be subtle and conform to a pastel palette of textbook shades, or they can be an expression of your own enthusiasm—a mix of bright colors in the style of a Monet painting

IT IS EVERY gardener's dream to have a colorful (herbaceous) border in flower for as long as possible—and so it is with clematis enthusiasts. Color, form and foliage are well satisfied with clematis through the year, but it is the mad rush of clematis growth from spring to autumn that stretches the imagination and requires some strategic planning. There are many combinations to be had with clematis: either a pink-blue, red-blue one or a yellow and blue mixture would be fine depending on your tastes.

Montanas are excellent together with straggly hedges and mature trees since they can climb up to 23ft. (7m.) and give contrast to otherwise dreary foliage such as leylandii (x *Cupressocyparis leylandii*), the white or pink flowers and the dark or light green foliage making a pleasant offering for the spring. Gertrude Jekyll employed *C. montana* on a large scale in her gardens, intertwining it with hazel (*Corylus avellanus*) and English holly (*Ilex aquifolium* A.G.M.) or growing it with European guelder rose (*Viburnum opulus*). She also combined *C.* 'Jackmanii' A.G.M. (only the clearer purple or cooler tones are recommended) with gray-leaved sea buckthorn (*Hippophae rhamnoides* A.G.M.). Montanas can also be grown with wisterias to good effect. Yet another effective combination is the climbing hydrangea (*Hydrangea petiolaris*) with *C. tangutica*, the yellow bells being complementary to the white, foamy flowers of the hydrangea. It is worth considering the dark foliage of *Pittosporum tenuifolium* 'Tom Thumb' A.G.M. as a foil for many of the large hybrids or, in reverse contrast, the mystical dark colors of *C. viticella* 'Purpurea Plena Elegans' A.G.M. against the light-colored, yellow form of black locust (*Robinia pseudoacacia* 'Frisia' A.G.M.).

C. 'Acton Splendour' and ceanothus
ABOVE *Growing clematis and ceanothus together might not appeal to many, but it can work to beautiful effect.*

C. montana and wisteria
LEFT *Wisteria and clematis are obvious companions and they do well together in each of their own color forms.*

C. 'Victoria' and day-lilies (*Hemerocallis*)
ABOVE *A striking duo in terms of color, purple clematis and yellow day-lilies make an eye-catching display.*

C. tangutica and Hydrangea petiolaris
LEFT *More subtle tones are entertained here with clematis and the filigree parts of hydrangea.*

C. maximo-wicziana, C. 'Bill MacKenzie' A.G.M. and eccremocarpus
LEFT *The interaction of the clematis with these tendril vines makes a striking tableau.*

C. 'Bill MacKenzie' A.G.M. seedling and C. x jouiniana 'Praecox' A.G.M.
LEFT *These two clamberers together provide differences in color, shape and form.*

C. 'Victoria' with *Thalictrum aquilegiifolium* 'Purple Cloud'
ABOVE *The purple flowers of 'Victoria' look wonderful against the delicate, fluffy, purple heads and green foliage of meadow rue.*

GROWING CLEMATIS

GROWING CLEMATIS can be extremely rewarding. A healthy specimen planted in the right soil conditions and with warm weather can burst into growth and produce a show of flowers within three months. In these circumstances, all the clematis grower need do is to sit back and enjoy the colorful display. Clematis, like other plants, are susceptible to some pests, diseases and deficiencies, but they have surprising resistance to many ailments and will thrive with a little attention. From planting, fertilising and watering clematis to propagating them and identifying pests and diseases when they strike, this chapter contains all the information necessary to cultivate healthy plants that will live up to all expectations.

C. macropetala
ABOVE *This is one of the easiest clematis to grow, because it is vigorous and needs no pruning.*

C. viorna
LEFT *The leather flower or vase vine, native to South America, is a species clematis with interesting, bell-shaped flowers.*

95

Planting

*All clematis will grow better if their roots and the lower part of the stem are kept
fairly cool. This can be achieved by mulching the soil surface or by planting a low-growing
plant close to the root ball to give added shade.*

WHEN PLANTING clematis, it is vital that the variety you have chosen will do well in the location you have selected. It is no good planting a clematis that likes a cool, shady site in a hot, sunny position and vice versa. You should also check to see what height the plant is likely to reach. Many hybrid clematis will grow to about 3–5ft. (1–1.5m.), although there are exceptions (see Clematis A–Z, pages 110–21 for height information on more than 350 clematis). When buying a clematis, choose one that looks strong and healthy, with new, young growth and a good root ball.

It is a good idea to dig the hole for the clematis before you buy one from a nursery. The clematis can then be planted immediately, rather than being left to languish in its pot. Every day counts when you first plant a clematis and you will be surprised what

growth is put on straight after planting. Taking the plant out of its nursery pot requires care, since it can collapse. Gently tap the base of the pot with your hand while holding the pot and its stakes with the other. Older plants may be more firmly interlaced with the base and holes of the pot. These can be eased out by cutting a few of the protruding roots. Transfer the entire contents of the container, with stakes and as much of the potting mix as possible, to the planting hole. Ensure that the bottom of the main stem of the clematis where it arises from the root ball is set about 2in. (5cm.) below the surface of the soil. This will help the clematis to grow better and keep the roots cool. Follow the same guidelines for planting clematis in containers. If the container is in full sun, mulch the soil or grow a sprawling sedum over the surface to reduce water loss.

Soaking the root ball
*Before preparing the hole for the clematis, it is a good
idea to soak the root ball in a pail of rainwater. If it is
a container-grown plant or one in a plastic pot, it should
be plunged into the water for at least half an hour.*

Digging the hole
*Dig a hole two to three times larger than the root ball
and clinging soil (about 2 x 3ft./60 x 100cm. deep). Fill
the bottom with pottery shards or sticks to a depth of
about 8in. (20cm.) to provide adequate drainage.*

Filling the hole
Gently back-fill the hole and tamp down with garden compost. Use home-produced compost or a suitable brand-name compost with essential nutrients. Add more compost as the material settles.

Watering a newly planted clematis
The plant will need plenty of water to help it on its way. If the garden compost is mounded up to make a circular dam around the plant, this can be filled with water and allowed to percolate down at its own rate.

PLANTING AGAINST WALLS, TREES OR POSTS

If planting clematis next to a wall, make sure that the hole is at least 10in. (25cm.)
from the base of the wall. This will allow the roots of the clematis to enjoy the conditions of the bed better
without being hindered by the foundation and a general lack of water close to a wall.
The clematis can be encouraged to run up a small stake or a trellis to its main support.
The same technique is useful for planting clematis next to a tree or post.

To encourage the clematis to grow up its main support, a strong bamboo cane or thick stake can be placed at an angle between the planting hole and the trunk of the host tree (or wall). Push the stake into the ground away from the root ball, so as not to cause any damage.

Use string or stem ties to gently tie in the existing clematis stems and new growth. In this way you can train the plant to clamber up the stake and then on to its supporting structure.

Fertilising and watering

*Clematis are prodigious drinkers and will prosper with regular
fertilising and watering. Container-grown clematis will require more frequent
watering and fertilising than those planted in borders.*

WHILE FERTILISING is beneficial for some clematis, it would be wrong to assume that all clematis need fertiliser. Usually, if you get the growing conditions right, then the plant will grow strongly, perform well and reward you with first-class flowers. This is provided that it is a species or hybrid with a known track record of vigor, such as 'Hagley Hybrid' or 'Comtesse de Bouchaud' A.G.M., or C. 'Jackmanii' A.G.M..

There is a school of thought that says if the hole dug for the clematis is large enough and if the base of the hole has been filled with sticks for good drainage and the remainder with garden compost, the plant will not need any fertiliser at all. The belief is that by looking after the roots of the plant, it will thrive quite naturally.

Indeed, in their natural habitat, clematis fare very well in what are often very poor conditions, so why should they not manage just as successfully without additional nutrients in the garden? My argument is that as so many hybrid clematis are such poor performers, a little fertiliser goes a long way in promoting a vigorous plant, particularly during periods of rapid growth. It may certainly help a lackluster plant—and it may assist a reasonably healthy plant to perform even better. With the exception of montanas, which are such vigorous growers anyway, it is probably worth fertilising clematis as soon as they are planted in order to help them become established.

Do not over-fertilise because this not only wastes fertiliser but may also have a detrimental effect on plant growth. It is better not to use artificial fertiliser if you wish to respect the environment, since wasted material drains off into water courses. If you do use it, do so in moderation and with care. Better still, make your own fertiliser, either by steeping animal dung or by creating a fertiliser liquid from fermenting the leaves of comfrey (*Symphytum officinalis*), or compost plant as it is appropriately called. A favorite brand-name product is tomato fertiliser,

Measuring out fertiliser
*Following the manufacturer's instructions, pour the
required amount of concentrated tomato fertiliser into
the plastic measuring cup.*

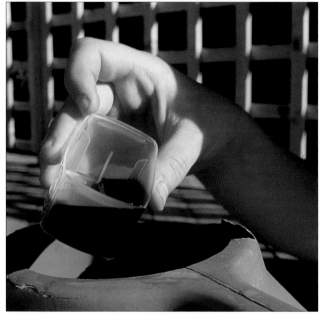

Diluting fertiliser
*Empty the concentrated fertiliser into a watering can
and dilute with water, according to the instructions.*

which should be diluted and given to plants once a week during summer. Another method is to place fertiliser pellets around the base of the plant. These are then released over a period of weeks through the action of rain or watering. This slow release of fertiliser helps to promote sustained growth. There are some who argue that fertilising clematis causes such great changes in terms of their vigor and performance that you would be hard-pressed to recognise your own plant. It does seem to be the case that the attributes of many wild clematis can be considerably improved in the garden environment.

The three essential components of any fertiliser are nitrogen (for growth), phosphate (for root development) and potash (for flowers and fruits). When planting a clematis it is useful to apply some phosphate in the hole before introducing the plant, so that the roots can be stimulated and encouraged to grow. Spring is a good time to fertilise clematis, since this will help them develop. Continue fertilising through late spring and summer to encourage strong plants and good flowers.

Most brand-name fertilisers also contain minor nutrients such as boron, magnesium, calcium and iron. However there is probably nothing quite so beneficial for the plants and the environment than home-produced fertiliser or taking care of the roots in the first place.

WATERING

When clematis are in an exposed position, in full sun or in soil that drains very quickly, they should be watered daily during spring and summer. The higher the compost content of the soil, the better the water retention. Adding mulching material to the soil surface will also help to retain water. Be wary of over-watering clematis, because the plants will die if they become waterlogged.

Adding fertiliser
Fertilise hungry clematis once a week in the morning or evening. Do not fertilise during the heat of the day, because this may cause damage to delicate root hairs.

Using slow-release fertiliser pellets
Pellets are ideal for containers, where the soil loses nutrients quickly. Sprinkle pellets on the soil surface so the fertiliser is released when the plant is watered.

Supports

In order to get the best from your clematis, it is very important to provide sufficient support. Clematis are much like fireworks in that they need to rise up rapidly before exploding into flowers.

SOME CLEMATIS need little encouragement to climb while others, even when given the best assistance, are sometimes reluctant, tardy or poor climbers. Their ability to scurry upward depends on their vigor—or lack of it—and whether the plant is strong, healthy and not restricted in any way. Some clematis are non-clinging, such as 'Aljonushka', 'Arabella' and *C.* x *eriostemon*, and their host is much more important to them in providing support.

Good performers are undoubtedly the montanas and the jackmanii clematis. They use their considerable powers of twisting leaf petioles to make very rapid progress up their hosts, curling around the stem every few inches and growing several inches in as many days. Montanas will snake up a tree in a matter of weeks, sending round a curving petiole every 4in.

(10cm.) or so with regular monotony until the summit is reached.

Another good group of performers are the armandii, which are probably the fastest growers in the clematis world after they break bud. These wonderfully plump buds burst forth in early spring, producing a shoot several yards long in just a few weeks. They will take to any support given, such as wooden doweling, wire or fencing, and will produce outward shoots if none is given. These performers simply need to be put on a framework or pillar for their energetic shoots to fall back on themselves and quickly form a floriferous pillar of color.

Whether you are growing clematis against a wall or tripod, arch or arbor or in a herbaceous border, some form of permanent or semi-permanent support is necessary. Wood is often

Pillar of
C. montana
LEFT *Established pillars of clematis are often self-supporting and need only general string attachments to stop them falling over in strong winds.*
INSET *A twining leaf stem curls itself around its support.*

Clematis smothering a trellis
ABOVE *Trelliswork is very useful behind clematis, since it offers many discreet opportunities to tie the plant.*

the preferred medium on which to grow clematis, since it mellows and is less intrusive than plastic tubing or netting. Wood trellis is a popular means of support for clematis. The trellis can be made or bought in various shapes and sizes to be fitted to a wall or made into a fence, which can then be used to form a compartment in the garden. Leading shoots of the clematis plant can then be tied to the trellis to help it progress. Gentle encouragement is all that is required before some of these vines take off and swamp a trellis or wall.

Another way of supporting a clematis up a wall or along a garden fence is to use eyes. These are screwed into the wood or brick and the clematis attached using twine or string. If the clematis is grown up a pillar or tripod, the shoots can be fed between alternating batons of wood, as you would do on a trellis, and all that is needed is to sit back and wait for the spectacular show.

Few people nowadays experiment with growing clematis as garlands suspended from gutters or walls, although the father of wild flower gardening, William Robinson, did just that at the turn of the 20th century. In the herbaceous border, the various herbaceous clematis—especially *C. x durandii* A.G.M., which has a particularly long flowering period—can be kept upright by growing them through other plants or be kept aloft with the help of small sticks.

Care is essential when handling clematis. They are extremely susceptible to breaking at their nodes (joints where the leaflets and flowers arise). This results in certain death to all parts of the flower around the break. Even relatively thick, woody stems are not immune to breakage as these, too, can snap or split in an instant. Caution should also be exercised when tying stem ties to clematis, since damage is just as easily caused at this stage.

C. viticella 'Mary Rose'
LEFT *'Mary Rose' makes good progress as a climber, even with little support.*

C. x durandii A.G.M.
RIGHT *This non-clinging, herbaceous clematis needs all the support you can give.*

C. armandii 'Snowdrift'
LEFT *Armandiis are mostly excellent growers but need frequent tying up.*

C. cirrhosa 'Freckles' A.G.M.
RIGHT *A good climber, it brings lots of flower bells.*

Pruning

*Pruning is not the knotty problem it is hyped to be if the gardener
understands the flowering habit of clematis. Beware of being too hasty in cutting out parts
that look dead, because these can suddenly spring into life if left to themselves.*

PRUNING CLEMATIS is not the thorny problem it is in roses. My philosophy is to allow the clematis to tell you when it needs to be pruned. Alpinas and macropetalas need little or no pruning at all and they are such delicate growers (though vigorous in their own sweet way) that it is a shame to cut away any part of them; they need judicious cutting back or restriction only to encourage them to cover as much vertical and lateral space as possible.

At the beginning of the new season, clematis will shoot from living stems. You can then cut back those parts farthest away from these points. During the dormancy period (winter), the stems of clematis look completely dead and will continue to look this way until just before they burst their buds. For this reason, it is important not to cut out clematis growth in the misapprehension that it has all died back. For any new clematis it is best not to prune in the first year and second year. Wait until the plant is established, see how it grows and determine the type of pruning necessary according to the pruning group to which the plant belongs.

There are three main pruning groups for clematis. Group 1 consists of species that flower early in the year on woody stems produced during

Clematis growing rampantly
ABOVE *When clematis is growing vigorously and is
not doing any harm, it is best left well alone.
Pruning may only serve to curb this delightful,
floriferous effect.*

Flower power
ABOVE *A good
show of flowers,
here on* C.
maximowic-
ziana, *is often
followed by lots
of dead flower
stalks, which
can be cut back.*

Snowed under
LEFT *Hardy
clematis can
survive through
harsh, winter
conditions.*

the previous year, such as alpinas and macropetalas. Group 2 includes all those clematis that flower in early summer, again on the previous year's woody stems, such as 'Belle of Woking', 'Marie Boisselot' A.G.M. and 'Mrs. George Jackman' A.G.M. Group 3 is made up of late summer- and autumn-flowering clematis, such as jackmanii and viticellas, that flower on the current year's growth (see box below). There is nothing quite like studying your clematis as they grow. Keeping pests and diseases at bay, removing bits of dead plant and untangling knotted stems that haven't been well-trained are typical jobs. One trick is to keep pinching back the central bud of a lead shoot. This will encourage it to produce two side buds. Do the same with the side buds after they have grown on, *ad infinitum.* This works wonders on viticellas, producing more growth, a bigger plant and delaying flowering.

Removing dead stems
LEFT *Dead and weak stems should be removed, along with dead leaves, in early summer, late winter or early spring, depending on when the clematis flowers (see below).*

Making the cut
LEFT *Prune the dead stems hard, reducing them down to the highest pair of healthy-looking leaf axil buds.*

PRUNING GROUPS

Some clematis flower on the previous year's woody stems, others on the current year's growth. This determines the type of pruning recommended. There are three basic pruning groups.

Group 1 (e.g. *C. alpina* 'Jacqueline du Pré')
Clematis in this group flower early in the year on stems produced during the previous year. Little pruning is required other than to train them and keep them within bounds. Enjoy their prolific flowers but do not cut away any of the previous year's growth.

Group 2 (e.g. *C. orientalis*)
Includes those that flower in early summer, again on woody stems produced in the previous year. These need to be pruned lightly in early spring since they are only a few weeks away from flowering, but they do need some of last year's growth removed, especially where it is dead. Check by breaking a piece of stem well away from the plant to see if it is green and healthy inside. If not, then it is dead at this extremity and may be removed.

Group 3 (e.g. *C.* 'Gipsy Queen' A.G.M.)
Includes the late summer- and autumn-flowering clematis that flower on the current year's growth. You can remove some of the old growth after flowering in autumn, since this will prevent the plant from being damaged in winter. This group are best pruned hard in early spring, when they are still many weeks away from flowering. Cut back to a pair of buds from where you would like the plant to burst forth, or at about the lowest set of buds from the ground.

Propagating

Propagating clematis is a fun, quick and inexpensive way of increasing pleasure in the garden. There are various means of propagation, the most popular of which are sowing seed and taking cuttings.

IN NATURE clematis are pollinated by a variety of natural sources, including butterflies and moths, flies and bumblebees. These are either attracted to the color or the smell of the plant and feed on the pollen in the flowers. Although some clematis produce pollen, very few form nectar. Old man's beard (*C. vitalba*) is one of the rare cases, presenting nectar as little droplets on its filaments—unlike most plants, which produce nectar at the base of their petals.

By moving from one plant to another (of the same species), the insects transfer the pollen from one plant to the female parts of the flower of another. Pollen arriving on a ripe female flower will germinate, effecting cross-pollination. Fertilisation will result in the growth of new seed, which will be identical to those of its parents. In greenhouses and polytunnels this cross-pollination can be controlled by clematis breeders. The breeder takes ripe pollen from one parent and places it on the female parts of the other chosen parent. This is a skilled process whereby the pollen is collected on the tip of a fine paintbrush and transferred to a freshly opened flower that has been kept insect-free. By isolating the flower under muslin, pollination cannot be interfered with and the breeder can guarantee that the seeds will reflect the parents.

Sowing seed is a rewarding way of growing clematis, but it does require patience. Fresh seed is often more successful than packeted seed and can be fluffy. This is because the "tails" or plumes that help to waft the seeds away in the wind are still

Natural pollination
LEFT *In the wild, bumble-bees and other insects help to transfer pollen between flowers.*

Controlled pollination
ABOVE *In controlled greenhouse conditions, muslin is placed over the plant to insure that insects do not interfere with cross-pollination.*

Fresh seed heads
LEFT *It is always worthwhile collecting seed heads from your own or friends' plants, because these often prove more successful than packeted seed.*

attached. Plant all parts of the seed, so you know where the seed is. Other seed is so fine or so close to the color of potting mix that it is difficult to keep track of it. Always place an identification name tag on the seed flat, along with the date. Once germinated, thin the seedlings when they are of manageable size and insert them into small pots. Allow the seedlings to grow on until they are 4–6in. (10–15cm.) high before potting them or planting in the garden. Growing the plants in pots enables them to become larger, stronger and less susceptible to attack from slugs.

Another way of propagating is to take a node of a well-established plant with a large mass of shoots arising from the node, and cut this off ³⁄₄in. (2cm.) from either side of the node. Plant this in a pot after cutting back all other shoots to about 2¹⁄₂in. (6cm.). Keep watered and look out for small roots to develop.

SOWING SEEDS

Growing clematis from seed can be very satisfactory—but be prepared for disappointments. Some seeds germinate rapidly and can be flowering within three months. Others will never come up, or take so many weeks or months that you miss the season you were growing them for.

1 Sprinkle fine seed on to a tray of seed starter mix, or, with large seeds, press them lightly into the mix.

2 Lightly tamp down the mix over the seeds.

3 After sowing, spray the starter mix with rainwater; then ensure that it is kept moist at all times.

4 After days or weeks, seedlings will emerge. Once they are of a size to be handled, thin them or replant them in individual pots.

TAKING CUTTINGS

By taking cuttings, you will be reproducing a replica of the parent plant, so choose a clematis that is strong and healthy for best results. Cuttings should be taken from the parent plant in late spring or early summer.

How to take cuttings

Cut sections from new, green growth and trim to a pair of buds, leaving ¹⁄₅in. (0.5cm.) above and 1¹⁄₂–2in. (4–5cm.) below. Dip the cut base into hormone powder and insert into cutting starter mix. Label and water.

Pests

Clematis leaves are sometimes eaten by caterpillars, and many are disfigured by leaf miners or cutter insects. Generally, clematis are not completely defoliated by insects as in many plants, so they have some degree of resistance.

CLEMATIS ARE not immune to the vagaries of insect pests and those grown in greenhouses are a little more susceptible to attack, because of the warmer conditions, than those grown outside, especially during the winter.

One of the most common pests is the caterpillar of a small moth called the Carnation tortrix moth, (*Cacoecimporpha prunubana*), which lives inside a rolled-up leaf while feeding. These rolls are easy to spot and are best removed and destroyed. The fully grown caterpillar turns into a chrysalis that hatches into a moth. A vacant leaf roll can be spotted by a half-protruding, pupal case from which the adult has flown. Moths mate and lay eggs on the leaves to renew the cycle again. Sometimes segments of the clematis leaf are eaten by leaf-cutting bees. There is little that can be done to control them but they are not a major problem. Aphids are a significant pest, causing the leaves and stems to become sticky and sooty and affecting the health of the plant. These are best dealt with by using a brand-name approved pesticide spray. Slugs eat seedlings, can destroy newly planted clematis seedlings overnight and strip the bark from a full-grown plant, giving it a whitish look. As a result, the plant may die from this grazed point outward. Slugs are best controlled by setting traps filled with stale beer to attract and drown them, or by using slug pellets. I am not keen on the latter, because they harm birds and small mammals that prey on slugs. Leaf miners leave trails on leaves that are disfiguring but not particularly harmful.

Carnation tortrix moth
LEFT AND FAR LEFT *The tiny caterpillar of the tortrix moth rolls up a leaf in which it hides from predators while feeding on it.*

Leaf-cutting bees
LEFT *Leaf-cutting bees eat parts of the leaf, but there is little that can be done to dissuade them from attacking clematis (or roses).*

Aphids
LEFT AND INSET *Aphids feed on the sap of young, tender clematis leaves and stems. The tiny holes become infected with bacteria and discoloration of the leaf occurs.*

Agromyzid fly
LEFT *Leaf miners, such as the caterpillar of the agromyzid fly, move between the upper and lower surfaces of the leaves, causing characteristic tracks.*

Slugs and snails
LEFT *At night, slugs and snails will strip clematis stems with their rasping mouthparts, giving them a whitish appearance.*

Phytomyza fly
RIGHT *These are the marks of the larva of the phytomyzid fly, which disfigure the leaves but do not do any great damage.*

Diseases

*Clematis are not especially prone to diseases but there are those, such as wilt,
that cause severe damage. Man's selected hybrids are weaker than true species clematis,
which have some natural resistance.*

MICRO-ORGANISMS that attack clematis include viruses, bacteria and fungi. Viruses cause color irregularities on leaves, while fungi include two important disease agents: *Ascochyta clematidina*, which gives rise to wilt; and *Phytophora* sp., which produces mildew. Mildew tends to affect jackmanii and texensis clematis and occurs in summer when there is high humidity in the garden. It can be controlled with a brand-name fungicidal spray. Fungi grow in dark, humid places, such as in an overgrown garden that never receives direct sunlight or is next to water. Wilt is widespread and can strike anywhere, even in sunny positions. Fungal spores are borne on the wind and it is unlikely that chemical methods suggested for eradicating them are very effective. Some clematis are more susceptible to wilt and these include new hybrids. Stick to species clematis that appear to be resistant or to herbaceous clematis for wilt-free clematis growing. The large-flowered hybrids are highly susceptible to wilt, especially those bred from *C. languinosa*. Wilt often only affects stems of the plant, and usually does not kill it. The same is true of another fungus called *Glomerella cingulata*, which causes anthracnose. This is a disease where the leaves become spotted and fall, and the stem collapses. Like wilt, plants usually send up new shoots, but it may then be too late for a good showing. A disease that has struck clematis in the mid- to late 1990s is called "slime flux". It is a bacterial disease of trees and has now included clematis among its hosts. The bacterium first causes the symptoms of wilt with yellowing of leaves. Then a smelly, white-pink fluid bleeds from the stem. Diseased plants need to be dug up and burned. Mineral deficiency is common, causing blotches of light color on leaves. Apply fertiliser containing nutrients such as iron.

Wilt in flowers
ABOVE *No disease is more distressing than wilt, which can strike overnight and lay waste to your most spectacular displays.*

Wilt in leaves
LEFT *When wilt strikes, leaves can wither and die within a few days.*

Mildew
BELOW *Mildew is a fungus that grows on all surfaces of the plant when conditions are hot and humid.*

Mineral deficiency

LEFT *Mineral deficiency causes the discoloration of leaves. It is sometimes confused with aphid feeding, which produces very similar symptoms.*

Yellowing of leaves

ABOVE *Seen here on a* C. vitalba *plant, yellowing leaves can be caused either by mineral deficiency or by drought conditions causing a breakdown of the green pigment.*

Virus attack

ABOVE *Viruses are numerous and can cause mottled or deformed leaves.*

Rust

LEFT *Rust is a fungus that reveals itself as a fine, granular growth on both leaves and stems.*

LEAF DIE-BACK

Armandiis often produce unsightly, brown leaves or sections of leaves. This is often caused by the plant giving up on some smaller shoots in favor of more successful longer ones. Patches of discoloration may be caused by a mineral deficiency.

Leaf die-back on armandii clematis is unsightly rather than life-threatening but there's little that can be done to prevent it. The best way to deal with it is to pluck out the badly affected leaves.

CLEMATIS
A–Z

T HIS COMPREHENSIVE directory lists more than 400 species and cultivars of clematis from around the world, arranged alphabetically. Names of breeders and when and where cultivars were bred are given where relevant, together with any inherited parental characteristics, the size and color of the flowers, flowering times, an indication of vigor and the pruning group to which each plant belong. All the clematis listed are considered to be hardy, that is they will reliably perform in a temperature range of -10 to -50°F (-23 to -46°C), unless marked with star symbol (*), which denotes that they are tender and will not survive if the the temperature falls below 0°F (-18°F). For USDA hardiness zone information, see the chart on page 122.

C. 'Fuji-musume'
ABOVE *A large-flowered clematis with striking, blue-purple sepals, this makes a good container plant for the patio.*

C. montana 'Tetrarose'
LEFT *Compact, pink flowers with a thick brush of yellow stamens make this vigorous plant ideal for growing over a pillar, in a hedge or mixed with* C.m.'Elizabeth' A.G.M.

111

Clematis A–Z

This comprehensive listing covers the most popular and attractive as well as some of the more unusual varieties of clematis. Figures in brackets denote the pruning group to which each clematis belongs. For more information on these groups, see pages 102–103.

'Abundance' This cultivar was raised by the Jackmans in the 1930s and the flowers are deep red with a yellow boss from mid- to late summer. Viticella Group. (3)

akebioides Now regarded as a true species, this was once a variety of *C. glauca*, a native of China. Its small, nodding, yellow flowers are to $1\frac{1}{2}$ in. (4cm.) across in mid-summer. (2)

'Alba Luxurians' A.G.M. Astonishing irregular patterns of whites and greens on the sepals is provided by this cultivar in mid-summer to early autumn. For best effect grow over a wall. Viticella Group. (3)

'Albiflora' Small, single white flowers are borne on this deciduous vine from mid- to late spring. It does well in containers, to $6\frac{1}{2}$–10ft. (2–3m.). Alpina Group. (1)

'Alice Fisk' Large, single blue flowers with brown stamens are produced in mid-season on a deciduous plant that grows $6\frac{1}{2}$–10ft. (2–3m.). Patens Group. (1)

'Allanah' Ruby-red sepals drawn out to wide spatula shapes make this a very attractive plant with flowers up to $5\frac{1}{2}$ in. (14cm.) in mid- to late summer. The light stamens are tipped in black. Jackmanii Group. (2)

alpina **A.G.M.** A species clematis with pale blue, single flowers scrambling to 10ft. (3m.). A spring flowerer, it can be grown in a container or through shrubs. In the wild there may be more foliage than flowers, while in cultivation there are often more flowers than foliage. (1)

alpina **'Columbine'** Small, pale blue, nodding flowers are borne in spring on a deciduous plant that grows to 10ft. (3m.). It is ideal for a container. (1)

alpina **'Constance'** A seedling from *alpina* 'Ruby', this deciduous plant has small, single, bright red flowers in spring, grows to 10ft. (3m.) and thrives up a trellis or in a container. (1)

alpina **'Francis Rivis' A.G.M. U.K. form** The largest of the alpina hybrids, this has pale blue flowers with fairly long sepals, flowers in spring and will grow up a wall or trellis or in a container, to 10ft. (3m.). (1)

alpina **'Francis Rivis' A.G.M. Dutch form** This has shorter sepals than the U.K. form and grows as above. (1)

alpina **'Frankie'** With its small, single, mid-blue flowers and blue-tipped anthers in spring, this plant tolerates any aspect and grows to 10ft. (3m.). (1)

alpina **'Helsingborg' A.G.M.** Fine, dark purple, single flowers are borne in spring on this scrambling, deciduous plant, which is ideal for growing through shrubs. (1)

alpina **'Jacqueline du Pré'** Single, pale pink, semi-nodding flowers are produced in spring on this deciduous climber with pale green foliage. (1)

C. 'Asao'

alpina 'Pamela Jackman' Single, small and deep blue flowers with yellow bosses are borne freely in spring on this scrambling plant. It grows well in a container or against a trellis and has short, stubby sepals. (1)

alpina 'Pink Flamingo' The strident pinkness of the sepals makes this scrambling, deciduous clematis distinctive. It grows to 10ft. (3m.), ideally through shrubs or in containers, and flowers in spring. (1)

alpina 'Rosy Pagoda' Single, pale pink flowers are borne in spring on a deciduous, scrambling plant to 10ft. (3m.). (1)

alpina 'Ruby' The rich ruby to pink of the sepals contrast attractively with the yellow to cream boss. It grows in a container to 6½ft. (2m.) and flowers in spring. (1)

alpina subsp. *sibirica* This is a subspecies of the true species *C. alpina* A.G.M., with white instead of blue to mauve sepals. It flowers in spring.(1)

alpina subsp. *sibirica* 'White Moth' This clematis has the long sepals of a U.K. form of a *C.* 'Francis Rivis' but they are all white with a white boss, very much like the wings of a ghost moth. It is a vigorous, spring-flowering species which will climb a trellis or wall to 10ft. (3m.). (1)

alpina 'Tage Lundell' Named after the Swedish clematis breeder, this has rich rose-purple, pointed sepals, will grow to 10ft. (3m.) and flowers in spring. (1)

alpina 'White Columbine' A.G.M. Small, single white flowers are borne in spring on a deciduous plant that grows to 10ft. (3m.). It is ideal for a container. (1)

alpina 'Willy' The single flowers are very pale pink and reddish toward the base of the sepals. It is deciduous, spring-flowering and grows to 10ft. (3m.). (1)

'Andromeda' Semi-double, pink-striped flowers are borne from late spring to early autumn. This deciduous plant will grow to about 12ft. (4m.). Later flowers may be single. Florida Group. (1)

'Anna' Large, pearly pink single flowers are borne in spring and late summer on this compact, deciduous plant that suits containers. Patens Group. (1)

'Anna Louise' ('Evithree') Large, red flowers with scarlet bars are borne in spring and late summer on a plant that grows to 10ft. (3m.). (1)

'Arctic Queen' ('Evitwo') Attractive, large, double white flowers are produced from spring to autumn. (1)

armandii A species clematis with long, evergreen leaves, this has white, scented flowers borne freely in spring as trusses along the stem. An extremely vigorous vine, it can grow to 33ft. (10m.). (1)

armandii 'Apple Blossom' The undersides of the sepals are a pale pink, rather like apple blossoms, and the flowers, borne in spring, are scented. A vigorous vine to 26ft. (8m.), it grows well up arbors, pillars or on a trellis. (1)

armandii 'Jeffries' This is a selection of the species with pointed leaflets, which bears numerous scented flowers in spring and sometimes flowers again, though less prolifically, in summer. (1)

armandii 'Snowdrift' This has scented, white flowers in spring and is a form of the species clematis. (1)

x *aromatica* Delicate in form and flower, this is a non-clinging hybrid between *C. flammula* and *C. integrifolia*. The flowers, borne in mid- to late summer, have tiny, well-separated, violet-purple sepals, a tuft of yellow stamens and a vanilla scent. (3)

'Asao' Large, pink-red flowers are seen from spring to early autumn, with pointed sepals and paler centers. It is

a deciduous plant to about 10ft. (3m.). Patens Group. (1)

'Ascotiensis' A.G.M. An older cultivar from 1874, the sepals are mid-blue, up to 5in. (13cm.) across, and the anthers dark brown. It flowers from mid- to late summer and is ideal in a container. Jackmanii Group. (3)

'Aureolin' A.G.M. This Dutch-raised, summer to early autumn-flowering cultivar has much larger flowers than the true species tangutica. It is just as vigorous and produces attractive seed heads. (2)

'Barbara Dibley' This has large, red flowers with a central, carmine band from mid- to late summer. It grows to 10ft. (3m.) and is deciduous. Best grown in sun. Patens Group. (1)

'Barbara Jackman' Large, mauve flowers borne in mid- to late summer have a crimson bar. The plant thrives in any aspect. Patens Group. (1)

'Beauty of Worcester' Double, deep blue flowers are produced early in the year, single ones in the autumn. It is best grown in sun. Florida and Lanuginosa Groups. (1)

'Bees' Jubilee' A.G.M. An attractive mid- to late summer-flowering hybrid with two-tone colors of mauve-pink and white. Patens Group. (1)

'Belle Nantaise' Growing to about 10ft. (3m.), this is a mid-season large-flowered cultivar with purple flowers and yellow stamens. It was raised in 1887 by Boisselot in France. Lanuginosa Group. (2)

'Belle of Woking' Large, silvery mauve, double flowers may be borne from spring to autumn. This vigorous hybrid grows to 10ft. (3m.). Florida and Lanuginosa Groups. (1)

'Betina' A deciduous plant bearing single, dark purple-red flowers in spring. It grows to 10ft. (3m.). Alpina Group. (1)

'Betty Corning' Pink, scented flowers up to 2½in. (6cm.) across are produced in summer to early autumn. It can grow to 6½ft. (2m.). Viticella and Texensis Groups. (3)

'Blue Bird' A Canadian cultivar raised by Frank Skinner in 1962, this has mauve-blue flowers up to 2½in. (6cm.) across. It flowers in spring and early summer. Macropetala Group. (1)

'Blue Boy' Raised in Canada in 1947, this hybrid between *C. viticella* and *C. integrifolia* has pale blue sepals and flowers in mid- to late summer. It will grow to about 6½ft. (2m.) and is deciduous. (3)

'Blue Dancer' Small, single light blue flowers with long sepals are borne prolifically in spring on a deciduous plant that reaches 10ft. (3m.). Ideal for a container. Alpina Group. (1)

'Blue Moon' ™ ('Evirin') Launched at the Chelsea Flower Show in 1997, this early large-flowered clematis bears pale lilac and white flowers up to 7in. (18cm.) across, often in two showings from late spring to early autumn. It has distinctive red anthers. (2)

'Blue Ravine' A 1970s North American hybrid from 'Nelly Moser' and 'Ramosa', this vigorous hybrid has large blue flowers from early summer to early autumn. It thrives in hot weather and grows to 10ft. (3m.). Patens Group. (2)

campaniflora A species clematis native to Portugal and Spain, this has white to palest blue flower "bells" borne on a vigorous plant in mid-summer. (3)

campaniflora 'Lisboa' Differing from the true species, this has larger, purple-blue flowers in mid-summer. (3)

'Carnaby' Large, single flowers are borne on compact, deciduous plants in mid-season. It will grow up to 10ft. (3m.) and is ideal for a container. Lanuginosa Group. (1)

'Charissima' Raised by Pennells and named in 1974,

this plant has cerise colored flowers up to 7in. (18cm.) across in two flushes from early summer to early autumn. It does well in sun or shade. Patens Group. (2)

chinensis * A true species clematis, native to China, this will grow to 13ft. (4m.) and produces masses of starry, white flowers in autumn. (3)

cirrhosa * A species clematis with clusters of very pale green flowers in early to mid-spring and evergreen, dark green foliage. (1)

cirrhosa var. *balearica* A.G.M. * Single, green flowers display purple-speckled throats in early to mid-spring. It has evergreen leaves and reaches 10ft. (3m.) on a trellis. (1)

cirrhosa 'Freckles' A.G.M. * The inside of the single flower is splashed in purple while the outside is a contrasting dusty caramel. It flowers in winter and the leaves are evergreen, as in all cirrhosas. (1)

cirrhosa 'Wisley Cream' * Small, bell-shaped, pale green to cream flowers are borne from late winter to early spring on a straggling plant that has shiny, evergreen leaves. It can miss a year of flowering. (1)

'Comtesse de Bouchaud' A.G.M. This delightful bearer of many pink flowers from mid-summer to autumn likes full sun and mixes well with roses. Jackmanii Group. (3)

'Corona' Purple-pink flowers up to 6in. (15cm.) across are borne from late spring to late summer on this compact cultivar raised in Sweden in the early 1970s. It flowers freely and is useful for cut flowers. Patens and Lanuginosa Groups. (2)

'Countess of Lovelace' This is one of those clematis that has double flowers in spring and then single ones in summer. The flowers are lilac-blue and the plant will grow to 10ft. (3m.). Patens Group. (1)

'Crimson King' Also known as 'Crimson Star', this is crimson and star-like. The flowers, to 7in. (18cm.) across, are borne from mid- to late summer. It was originally raised by Jackmans in 1915. Lanuginosa Group. (3)

x *cylindrica* A hybrid clematis from *C. crispa*, this has upstanding, open bell flowers in purple to rose-mauve in mid-summer. The sepals twist around their axis, making it distinctive. (3)

'Daniel Deronda' A.G.M. Large, semi-double, violet-blue flowers are seen in summer, single ones later. Patens Group. (1)

'Dawn' Large, pearly pink flowers and contrasting, red stamens are produced from late spring to early autumn. Grow out of shade to maintain flower color. Lanuginosa and Patens Groups. (1)

'Doctor Ruppel' A.G.M. Striking flowers with broad, pointed sepals in red-purple with pink edges are borne from late spring to early autumn on a deciduous plant growing to 13ft. (4m.). Patens Group. (1)

'Dorothy Walton' Once called 'Bagatelle', this has blue to mauve flowers to 4³/₄in. (12cm.) in early to late summer and is a good container plant. Jackmanii Group. (3)

'Duchess of Albany' A.G.M. The soft pink, tubular flowers appear from mid-summer to autumn. It was raised in 1890 by Jackman, who crossed *C. texensis* with *C.* 'Star of India' A.G.M. Texensis Group. (3)

'Duchess of Edinburgh' Medium-sized, double white flowers, like plump rosettes, are borne in early summer and semi-double ones later. In early development, the double flowers' sepals are all green. The stamens are yellow. Florida Group. (1)

'Duchess of Sutherland' Distinctive, large mauve-red

flowers and contrasting yellow stamens are borne from early summer to early autumn on a plant growing to 10ft. (3m.). Viticella and D Groups. (1)

x *durandii* A.G.M. One of the best and most widespread herbaceous clematis, this was raised in France in 1874. It needs other plants for support but its blue flowers, borne in summer and early autumn, are well worth having. (3)

'Edith' A.G.M. Large, single, white flowers are produced in summer on a deciduous plant that can grow to 16ft. (5m.). It is a seedling of 'Mrs. Cholmondeley'. (1)

'Edouard Desfossé' Raised more than 100 years ago by a French nursery of the same name, this hybrid has pale blue flowers up to 4³/₄in. (12cm.) across from late spring to early summer. Patens Group. (2)

'Edward Prichard' Raised in Australia with heracleifolia and recta parentage, this produces cream flowers from mid-summer to early autumn. Grow in full sun to gain the full benefit from its scented flowers. (3)

'Elsa Späth' A.G.M. A mid- to late summer-flowering clematis, this is a cultivar raised in Germany in 1891 with large lavender-blue sepals and chocolate-red stamens. Patens and Lanuginosa Groups. (2)

'Emilia Plater' The mauve sepals of this cultivar have a twist in them, are slightly reflexed and have a distinctive, dark purple bar. It flowers from summer to early autumn. Viticella Group. (3)

'Empress of India' Large, rose-red flowers to 7in. (18cm.) across are borne in summer and are suitable for cutting. The plant reaches 10ft. (3m.). Patens Group. (2)

'Entel' Viticella-like, this medium-sized flower has reflexed and ruffled pale mauve sepals and a boss of yellow-green stamens. It flowers in late summer. (2)

x *eriostemon* Produced as a hybrid between *C. integrifolia* and *C. viticella*, this has blue flowers whose sepals are reflexed backward. Good for scrambling about borders, it needs to be secured on arbors since it is non-clinging. It flowers from mid-summer to early autumn. (3)

'Ernest Markham' A.G.M. A popular cultivar with red-purple sepals and a large boss of yellow stamens, this plant loves sun and flowers from mid-summer to autumn. Jackmanii and Viticella Groups. (2)

'Etoile de Malicorne' The lavender-purple, late spring to late summer flowers are unusual because they are slightly reflexed upward in a cup shape. The large boss comprises light filaments and red anthers. Patens Group. (2)

'Etoile Rose' This is a valuable plant for any herbaceous border, since it grows to about 10ft. (3m.) and can be smothered in small, tulip-shaped, pink flowers in summer and early autumn. Texensis Group. (3)

'Etoile Violette' A.G.M. A French cultivar raised by Morel in 1885, this will smother a trellis or arbor with its small, violet-purple flowers from mid-summer to early autumn. Viticella Group. (3)

'Evening Star' ('Evista') This attractive border and container hybrid was produced in 1997. It has large red, purple, and mauve flowers with a dull yellow boss, borne from early to late summer and is susceptible to wilt. (2)

'Fair Rosamond' This is an off-white cultivar, flowering from mid- to late summer, with dark stamens, overlapping sepals and a scent of violets. It is ideal for containers. Patens and Lanuginosa Groups. (2)

'Fairy Queen' A mid- to late summer-flowering clematis with large flowers up to 7¹/₂in. (19cm.) across, which are palest pink with strident pink bars along the sepals. It

C. 'Countess of Lovelace'

has chocolate-tipped stamens. Lanuginosa Group. (2)

'Fireworks' A.G.M. A large splash of color is presented by the large summer flowers of this deciduous hybrid. The sepals are a two-tone, deep red in the center with carmine-pink on the outside. Patens Group. (1)

flammula The pure white clematis from the Mediterranean is a late summer- to autumn-flowering species, which comes into its own when *C. vitalba* fades. Both have masses of small, scented, star-like flowers. (3)

'Floralia' Pale blue sepals make up this Swedish cultivar raised by Magnus Johnson. It has reddish flower stalks and flowers in spring. Macropetala Group. (1)

florida **'Alba Plena'** An unusual clematis comprising bundles of overlapping, green sepals that open to become distinctive, pale green, double flowers from early summer to early autumn. (2)

florida **'Sieboldii'** The colors of this hybrid are reversed from the normal with its huge purple and lavender mix of stamens contrasting splendidly with uniform white sepals. It flowers from early summer to early autumn. (2)

'Fuji-musume' Raised in Japan in 1952, this produces sky blue flowers up to $5\frac{1}{2}$in. (13cm.) across in two flushes, from late spring to early summer. (2)

'Général Sikorski' A.G.M. Large, single mid-blue flowers with golden stamens are produced from mid- to late summer on this deciduous plant. Lanuginosa Group (1)

'Gillian Blades' A.G.M. Large, single white flowers with a hint of yellow in the center are borne in mid- to late summer on this deciduous hybrid. Patens Group. (1)

'Gipsy Queen' A.G.M. This seductive, dark velvety purple flowerer has dark purple stamens. It can grow to 16ft. (5m.) and will produce flowers from mid-summer to early autumn on the previous year's as well as the current year's growth. Jackmanii Group. (3)

'Glynderek' Double, deep blue flowers typify this early autumn-flowering hybrid, which can grow to 10ft. (3m.). Lanuginosa Group. (1)

gracilifolia This species clematis, with its small, white flowers and yellow stamens, blooms in late spring to early summer. It can be grown in most sunny aspects and reaches about 10ft. (3m.). (1)

'Gravetye Beauty' One of the reddest clematis ever bred, this was raised by Morel in France in about 1900, but introduced by expert William Robinson and named after his house, Gravetye. It flowers in summer and early autumn. Texensis Group. (3)

'Guernsey Cream' Creamy yellow flowers in late spring to late summer are typical of this well-named hybrid. It produces lots of flowers but the colors fade in direct sunshine. Patens Group. (1)

'Hagley Hybrid' One of the world's most popular clematis, this pink cultivar was introduced in 1956 by Jim Fisk. Remarkable for its ability to produce lots of flowers from early to late summer, its compact growth makes it ideal for containers. Jackmanii Group. (3)

'Haku-Ôkan' A distinctive hybrid with rich blue-purple

sepals, creamy boss and pale underside which flowers from late spring to early autumn. The sepals are pointed and their edges slightly rippled. Lanuginosa Group. (1)

'Helios' Raised in Holland, this cultivar has yellow flowers. Compact and not very vigorous, it flowers from mid-summer to early autumn and is suitable for containers and even hanging baskets. Tangutica Group. (2)

'Henryi' A.G.M. The pure whiteness of the sepals is outstanding in this popular, mid-season cultivar, first raised in Scotland in 1870. The stamens have a hint of purple. (2)

heracleifolia* var. *davidiana A herbaceous clematis that dies down in winter, this has scented, hyacinth-blue flowers in the axils of its large leaf stems from mid-summer to early autumn. It can be grown in any aspect. (3)

'H.F. Young' A.G.M. With its single flowers in mid-blue shades, this is one of the bluest clematis. It has cream stamens and flowers in late spring to late summer. A compact plant, it is ideal for a container. Lanuginosa/Patens Groups. (1)

'Horn of Plenty' A.G.M. This large, early summer and autumn-flowering clematis has rosy-purple sepals with a dark bar, and purple stamens. Patens and Lanuginosa Group. (2)

'Huldine' This classic clematis flowers from late summer to late autumn and is best grown in full sun against a wall. Viticella Group. (3)

'Hybrida Sieboldii' Growing best in full sun, this large-flowered clematis has pale blue flowers with red anthers from summer to early autumn. Jackmanii Group. (2)

integrifolia A true species clematis and a herbaceous one, native to Europe and Asia, it has bell-shaped flowers from mauve- to deep purple in early summer and early autumn. It demonstrates much variation in color and various forms are available. (3)

***integrifolia* 'Alba'** Highly variable, white forms exist and some are scented. They flower, like the other integrifolias, from early summer to early autumn. (3)

***integrifolia* 'Pangbourne Pink'** Selected from *C.i.* 'Rosea' A.G.M. by Denis Bradshaw in Kent, England, this pink form flowers from early summer to early autumn. (3)

'Jackmanii' A.G.M. Probably the most famous clematis, raised by the Jackmans in 1858. Its prolific, nodding flowers are purple, up to 4in. (10cm.) across, from early summer to early autumn. The plant is susceptible to wilt, but is very hardy in winter. (3)

'Jackmanii Alba' The white version of the purple 'Jackmanii' A.G.M., this has semi-double flowers in early summer and single flowers in mid-summer and autumn. (2)

'Jackmanii Rubra' Larger than the 'Jackmanii' A.G.M., this cultivar is enriched with red on its sepals and flowers from summer to early autumn. Jackmanii Group. (3)

'James Mason' Single, large white flowers with maroon stamens make this a spectacular clematis. It flowers from mid- to late summer and grows to 10ft. (3m.). (1)

'Jan Pawel II' Large, ivory-white flowers with overlapping sepals are borne from early summer to early autumn on a vigorous vine. The sepals may have a pink bar late in the year. Jackmanii Group. (1)

'John Huxtable' For purity of white this is a good contender, with its large flowers borne on a sturdy plant from mid- to late summer. It arose as a seedling from 'Comtesse du Bouchard', which it closely resembles. Jackmanii Group. (3)

'John Warren' The palest pink-gray colors of this early large-flowered clematis are unmistakable. Three stronger pink bars run the length of the sepals. The plants are compact and flower from early summer to early autumn. Lanuginosa Group. (2)

x *jouiniana* 'Praecox' A.G.M. The parents of this cultivar are *C. vitalba* and *C. heracleifolia*, which have both given characteristics to this useful border plant. It is rampant and floriferous, with small clusters of white-pink flowers from early summer to early autumn. (2)

'Kacper' One of the largest of all clematis, the deep purple flowers are up to 9in. (23cm.) across in two flushes from late spring to early autumn. Lanuginosa Group. (2)

'Kakio' Also called 'Pink Champagne', this Japanese cultivar is an early flowerer with large pink flowers to 6in. (15cm.) across. It is compact, so good in containers. (1)

'Kardynal Wyszyński' Crimson in color, this was raised by Brother Stefan in Poland and introduced by Jim Fisk in 1989. Its flowers, up to $4^3/_4$in. (12cm.) in diameter, are borne from mid-summer to autumn. Jackmanii Group. (3)

'Kathleen Dunford' Semi-double, large, rosy purple flowers turn to single flowers in autumn. Florida Group. (1)

'Kathleen Wheeler' From early summer to early autumn, large, single flowers of red-mauve with cream stamens are borne on a vigorous plant which can reach up to 13ft. (4m.). Patens Group. (1)

'Ken Donson' A.G.M. An early large-flowered clematis, this has dark blue sepals and yellow anthers. It was raised by Pennells in Lincoln, England and is useful as cut flowers or in a patio container. Lanuginosa Group. (2)

'Kermesina' Bright red colors suffuse the sepals, which each have a white patch at their bases. The clematis flowers from mid-summer to autumn. Viticella Group. (3)

'King Edward VII' Raised by Jackman in 1902, this cultivar has mauve flowers, a color associated with royalty. Its boss is made up of white filaments and pale purple anthers. It flowers from early to late summer and may grow to $6^1/_2$ft. (2m.). Lanuginosa Group. (3)

'Lady Betty Balfour' The purple-blue flowers may be up to 6in. (15cm.) across and, unusually for a hybrid, are produced in autumn. The flower color fades, the plant is susceptible to wilt and can be caught by autumn frosts, so beware. Jackmanii and Viticella Groups. (3)

'Lady Caroline Nevill' Semi-double flowers of a lavender-mauve hue are produced in early summer , followed by single flowers in mid- to late summer. It is a vigorous and free-flowering hybrid. (1)

'Lady Londesborough' Medium-sized, single flowers of a lavender-mauve color, with maroon-tipped stamens, are borne in late spring to early summer. Patens Group. (1)

'Lady Northcliffe' Flowering from early to late summer, this blue-flowered cultivar is compact and worthy of any container. Lanuginosa Group. (2)

'Lasurstern' A.G.M. A free-flowering hybrid with dark purple flowers and cream stamens from early to late summer, the translation 'Azure star' describes it well. Patens Group. (2)

'Lemon Chiffon' This has medium-sized, creamy white flowers with a touch of yellow and yellow stamens from late spring to early summer. It grows to 10ft. (3m.) and dislikes full sun. Patens Group. (1)

'Liberation' (Evifive) Characterised by its large, single flowers with narrow, red sepals and thick, cerise bars, this is a strident clematis growing to 6½ft. (2m.). It flowers from late spring to early summer. (1)

'Lilacina Floribunda' This is a late-flowering, large cultivar with deep purple flowers up to 4¾in. (12cm.) across, raised in England in 1880. It grows to about 10ft. (3m.). Lanuginosa Group. (3)

'Lilactime' Striking, semi-double flowers of wisteria-blue and magenta stamens are borne in spring. (1)

'Lincolnshire Lady' Raised by Valley Clematis Nursery, Lincolnshire, England, the bluish flowers to 2¾in. (7cm.) long are produced in spring and are paler toward the center. Macropetala Group. (1)

'Lincoln Star' Star-like qualities of this hybrid are enhanced by its pointed sepal shape. The medium-sized flowers are deep pink in the center, paler on the edges and appear from late spring to early autumn. Stamens are deep maroon. Patens Group. (1)

'Little Nell' This 1915 French cultivar has bluish white, small flowers, up to 2in. (5cm.) across from mid-summer to early autumn. Viticella Group. (3)

'Lord Nevill' A.G.M. Flowering in spring, summer and early autumn, this has deepest blue sepals with crenulated edges. Anthers are brownish. Patens Group. (1)

'Louise Rowe' Medium-sized, pale mauve single, semi-double and double flowers can be produced at the same time in spring, summer and early autumn. It grows to about 10ft. (3m.). Florida Group. (1)

macropetala This is the species clematis from China and Siberia that has produced so many varieties. Its lavender-blue flowers are semi-double and produced in large numbers in spring. (1)

macropetala **'Maidwell Hall' A.G.M.** The spring flowers of this cultivar, named after a hall in Northamptonshire, England are deeper blue than the normal. It can be planted in any aspect and will grow to 8ft. (2.5m.). (1)

macropetala **'Anders'** Raised in Sweden by Magnus Johnson, this cultivar has lavender-blue flowers up to 2in. (5cm.) long and flowers in spring. (1)

macropetala **'Ballet Skirt'** This spring-flowering cultivar has palest rose-white sepals and a boss of palest yellow. (1)

macropetala **'Harry Smith'** Named after a professor from China, who introduced this cultivar to Sweden in 1922, this cultivar has pale lavender flowers up to 1½in. (4cm.) long in spring. It is a good flowerer. (1)

macropetala **'Jan Lindmark'** Jan Lindmark raised this cultivar in Sweden before it was introduced to Britain by Raymond Evison in 1983. It has mauve-purple flowers and is one of the first spring flowerers. (1)

macropetala **'Lagoon'** The deepest blue of all the macropetalas, its spring flowers are up to 2½in. (6cm.) long and it tends to flower later than most cultivars. (1)

macropetala **'Markham's Pink' A.G.M.** Ernest Markham of Gravetye Manor, Sussex, England raised this cultivar in 1935. It has broad, pink sepals and flowers in spring. (1)

macropetala **'White Swan'** Raised in Canada by Frank Skinner in 1961, this has creamy white flowers to 2½in. (6cm.) long in late spring. It grows to 6½ft. (2m.) (1)

'Madame Baron Veillard' This vigorous cultivar produces lilac-rose flowers up to 4¾in. (12cm.) across in autumn, so needs a sunny position to prosper. It was raised by Veillard in 1885. Jackmanii Group. (3)

'Madame Edouard André' A.G.M. Flowering from mid-

C. 'Lasurstern'

to late summer, this compact plant is ideal for a container on a deck or patio. Its flowers are dark red with yellow anthers. Jackmanii Group. (3)

'Madame Grangé' A.G.M. This was raised by Grangé in France in 1875 and has the peculiar feature of the flowers not entirely opening. Velvet-purple with a red bar, they are produced in quantity in mid- to late summer. The plant grows to 10ft. (3m.). Jackmanii Group. (3)

'Madame Julia Correvon' A.G.M. An old favorite from France, this is ideal at the back of a herbaceous border with other clematis and producing waves of purple colors from mid-summer to early autumn. Viticella Group. (3)

'Margaret Hunt' Introduced by Jim Fisk in 1969, this is a vigorous vine to 10ft. (3m.), producing mauve-pink flowers from mid- to late summer. Jackmanii Group. (3)

'Margot Koster' Rich pinks are exhibited by this mid-summer clematis, whose sepals are usually gappy toward their base. With such clarity of color, it is bound to dominate borders. Viticella Group. (3)

'Marie Boisselot' A.G.M. Ideal for the side of a gate, this large-flowered, early to late summer-flowering cultivar can make a spectacle when scores of its flowers open simultaneously. Lanuginosa Group. (2)

'Marie Louise Jensen' Stunning flowers have four rich purple sepals, wavy on the edges, and a large boss with white-rose stamens in mid-summer. Jackmanii Group. (1)

'Masquerade' Introduced in 1993 by Raymond Evison, this cultivar is of unknown origin. It has blue-mauve flowers up to 7in. (18cm.) across and flowers from late spring to summer. Viticella Group. (1)

'Maureen' Growing to 10ft. (3m.), the velvety purple sepals are stunning at first but soon fade. Raised in 1955, it flowers in early to late summer. Lanuginosa Group. (2)

maximowicziana A North American species clematis, this is also known as *C. terniflora*. It is very vigorous and has masses of small, star-like white flowers in autumn, hence its common name of 'sweet autumn clematis'. (1)

'Minuet' A.G.M. The small, semi-nodding, white-purple flowers are produced *en masse* and look very attractive when the plant is grown over gates, through shrubs or into trees. It flowers in mid-summer. Viticella Group. (3)

'Miss Bateman' A.G.M. Raised in the 1860s by Charles Noble, this has white scented flowers up to 6in. (15cm.) across in late spring and mid-summer. Patens Group. (1)

'Miss Crawshay' Semi-double, pink-mauve flowers to 5in. (13cm.) are borne from early summer. Single flowers tend to be produced in late summer. Patens Group. (1)

montana The species clematis, native to China, is a vigorous vine to 33ft. (10m.), with masses of white scented flowers that turn pink with age. (1)

montana 'Alexander' * A white cultivar introduced by Colonel Alexander, this has large white flowers up to 2½ in. (6cm.) across in mid- to late spring and larger than normal leaves. It likes a sunny position. (1)

montana 'Broughton Star' * Double pink flowers are borne from mid- to late spring on this vigorous vine, which grows to 16ft. (5m.). It was raised by the Dennys of Preston, England in 1988. (1)

montana 'Continuity' * This vigorous hybrid has rich pink flowers opening from deep pink buds and large yellow anthers. It flowers almost continuously from early summer to early autumn, hence its name. (1)

montana 'Elizabeth' A.G.M. * The exquisite, single, pale pink flowers are seen in mid- to late spring. Their scent is variously described as vanilla and chocolate. (1)

montana 'Freda' A.G.M. * Like many montanas, the young foliage has a bronze coloring that turns green with age. The flowers are deep pink with a dark edge to the sepals. It can be grown in any aspect. (1)

montana f. *grandiflora* A.G.M. * Vigorous to 33ft. (10m.), the mid- to late spring flowers are pure white and a minimum of 2¾ in. (7cm.) across, though the largeness of the flowers seems to have been lost temporarily in cultivation. (1)

montana 'Marjorie' * Myriad semi-double flowers are produced during late spring and early summer. A vigorous plant, it does well over pergolas. (1)

montana 'Mayleen' * Soft baby pink flowers are borne in early to mid-summer, producing a vanilla scent. The boss is relatively large and the stamens are yellow. (1)

montana 'Mrs Margaret Jones' * This early 1990s cultivar has semi-double white flowers produced on a not so vigorous stock from late spring to early summer. (1)

montana 'Odorata' * Named after its sweetly scented, pale pink flowers, this cultivar is vigorous to 33ft. (10m.), flowers from mid- to late spring and can be grown in any aspect. (1)

montana 'Picton's Variety' * A compact cultivar raised by Percy Picton in the 1950s, this has mauve-pink flowers in mid- to late spring, grows to about 13ft. (4m.) and is regarded as a variety of *C.m.* 'Rubens'. (1)

montana 'Pink Perfection' * Similar to 'Elizabeth' A.G.M. but with pinker flowers in mid- to late spring. It is scented and will grow to 33ft. (10m.). (1)

C. 'Minuet'

montana var. *rubens* A.G.M. * This is meant to have rose-red flowers but many dark pink cultivars are now sold under this name. The original variety was introduced by Ernest Wilson from China earlier in the 20th century. It flowers in mid- to late spring. (1)

montana 'Tetrarose' A.G.M. * This clematis has lilac-rose flowers in mid- to late spring and bronzy foliage. It can be grown in any aspect and climbs to 33ft. (10m.). (1)

montana 'Vera' * A vigorous vine to 33ft. (10m.) with pink flowers to $2^3/_4$ in. (7cm.) across and a yellow mass of stamens in mid- to late spring. Strongly scented, it was raised in Cornwall earlier in the 20th century. (1)

montana 'Warwickshire Rose' The mid- to late spring flowers of this cultivar are palest pink, about $1^1/_2$ in. (4cm.) across, with a white-green mass of stamens. (1)

montana var. *wilsonii* * Noted for its twisted, small, white sepals, there is some dispute as to whether this cultivar, introduced by Ernest Wilson in the 1900s, is scented or not. It flowers from late spring to early summer. (1)

'Moonlight' Uniform and symmetrical, this pale yellow clematis was also called 'Yellow Queen'. Its flowers, in spring, summer and early autumn, are up to 7in. (18cm.) across. Patens Group. (2)

'Mrs. Bush' This mid-season large-flowered cultivar has lavender-blue flowers up to 8in. (20cm.) in diameter but is not free-flowering. Lanuginosa Group. (2)

'Mrs. Cholmondeley' A.G.M. A favorite with many, the large, pale blue flowers, up to 17in. (8cm.) across, are seen from spring to early summer It does well in a container. It was raised by Noble in 1873. Lanuginosa Group. (1)

'Mrs. George Jackman' A.G.M. Named after the Jackmans and raised by them in the 19th century, this cultivar produces semi-double flowers in early summer and singles in late summer. The flowers are creamy white and are produced prolifically. Patens Group. (1)

'Mrs. Hope' With pale blue sepals and red anthers, this is an attractive clematis cultivar. It flowers from spring to early autumn and does best in full sun. (2)

'Mrs. N. Thompson' A striking flower of bright purple with a deeper purple bar, the boss is large with white filaments tipped in pale purple. Raised by Pennells in 1961, it is an early large-flowered cultivar. Patens Group. (1)

'Mrs. P.B. Truax' This blue cultivar was raised by the Jackmans of Woking, England and, being of compact growth, is ideal for containers. Its flowers, borne in spring, summer and early autumn, are up to $4^3/_4$ in. (12cm.) across. Patens Group. (1)

'Multi Blue' In late spring and late summer, this has double or semi-double flowers that are of a unique structure. It is derived from a natural sport of 'The President' found in Holland in 1983. (1)

'Myôkô' Velvety red-purple flowers about 6in. (15cm.) across are seen from late spring to early summer on this Japanese cultivar. The yellow-cream boss is pronounced. It grows well in containers. Patens Group. (1)

napaulensis A species clematis native to northern India, the winter flowers are creamy white and $3/_4$ in. (2cm.) across. (1)

'Nelly Moser' A.G.M. One of the most popular of all clematis, this was raised just over 100 years ago by Moser in France. The late spring and early autumn flowers are large, up to 18cm (7in) across, and the white-pink sepals

have prominent purple bars. Lanuginosa and Patens Groups. (1)

'Nikolai Rubstov' The large pale pink flowers of this Ukrainian hybrid between 'Jackmanii' and 'Nelly Moser' are produced from late summer to mid-autumn. It can grown in any aspect to about 10ft. (3m.). (3)

'Niobe' A.G.M. An increasingly popular and widespread cultivar, this was raised in Poland and introduced by Jim Fisk in 1975. It has striking, dark red, velvet sepals and a large boss of yellow stamens, flowering from late spring until autumn. Jackmanii Group. (3)

orientalis A species clematis from Iran eastward to the Himalayas, this is one of the prettiest clematis. Its bells of small, yellow flowers are produced in summer. (2)

'Pagoda' Crossing *C. viticella* with *C.t.* 'Etoile Rose' is what John Treasure did to produce this cultivar in the 1970s. Its pink sepals, seen in summer and early autumn, are reflexed into a pagoda shape. Texensis Group. (3)

patens A species clematis native to China, this has flowers that vary from violet to white in early summer and early autumn. It is a woody vine and can grow to 13ft. (4m.). (1)

'Pennell's Purity' Looking more like a camellia or rose than a clematis, this double white cultivar has stunning reflexed and twisted sepals. It flowers in early summer. Lanuginosa Group. (2)

'Perle d'Azur' A.G.M. Introduced over 100 years ago by Morel in France, this free-flowering cultivar is popular because of its profusion of flowers from early summer to autumn. It can succumb to mildew. Jackmanii Group. (3)

'Perrin's Pride' Raised in New York State, this has large, rich purple flowers up to 6in. (15cm.) across. It flowers from early summer to autumn on the previous year's and current year's growth. Jackmanii Group. (3)

'Petit Faucon' Produced as a seedling from 'Daniel Deronda', this was introduced by Raymond Evison in 1989. From early summer to early autumn it has deep blue flowers with a yellow boss, which are up to $3^1/_2$ in. (9cm.) across, and will grow to 3ft. (1m.) It needs support since it is non-clinging. (3)

'Peveril Pearl' A selection from Barry Fretwell, this has lavender flowers up to 7in. (18cm.) across. It is a mid-season large-flowered clematis, which makes good cut flowers. Patens Group. (1)

'Pink Fantasy' A Jim Fisk introduction of 1975, this cultivar flowers from mid-summer to autumn. Its pink sepals are wide and pointed with a dark strawberry-red bar along the base . A compact plant, it is suitable for cut flowers or for containers. Jackmanii Group. (3)

pitcheri Native to central and south U.S.A., this species clematis is a good climber with purplish flowers from early summer to early autumn. (3)

'Polish Spirit' A.G.M. Raised by Brother Stefan in Poland in 1989, this cultivar has proved very successful. Of vigorous habit, it flowers in mid-summer to early autumn and is ideal for growing through trees and shrubs. Viticella Group. (3)

potaninii var. *fargesii* A species clematis native to China, this widespread, deciduous climber carries small, white flowers that look good when contrasting with a dark host plant. It flowers from mid-summer to early autumn. (3)

'Prince Charles' Popular as a trellis plant, the mid-summer to early autumn nodding mauve flowers are good value, though it can be susceptible to mildew. Jackmanii Group. (3)

'Proteus' A clematis with three different flower forms—double, semi-double and single—the flowers are up to 8in. (20cm.) across. It was raised by Charles Noble in 1876 and its range of pink, purple, green and yellow flowers are seen in spring, summer and early autumn. (1)

recta A species clematis from Europe, this herbaceous plant, to 5ft. (1.5m.), needs support but is valued for its many white, star-like fragrant summer flowers. (3)

recta 'Purpurea' The true species will always produce a small percentage of purple-stemmed individuals, and this is a typical example.It flowers in mid-summer. (3)

rehderiana A.G.M. Native to China, this has dull yellow flowers borne in clusters in midsummer on a very vigorous plant, which can grow to 23ft. (7m.) The flowers are bell-shaped. This species can be grown in trees. (3)

'Richard Pennell' A.G.M. Raised in 1974 by Pennell, this has bright purple-blue flowers up to 7in. (18cm.) across. It is an early large-flowered cultivar flowering from early summer to autumn. Patens Group. (1)

'Rosie O'Grady' A Canadian cultivar raised by Frank Skinner in 1964 with mauve-pink sepals up to 2³⁄₄in. (7cm.) long. Typical of the macropetalas, it can reach 10ft. (3m.). Macropetala Group. (1)

'Rouge Cardinal' An aristocratic clematis, this relatively new cultivar was raised by Girault in France in 1968. The flowers have deep red-purple sepals and a boss of off-yellow filaments and rose anthers. It flowers from mid-summer to autumn. Jackmanii Group. (3)

'Royal Velours' A.G.M. Dusky and dark, its impressive, red flowers, borne from summer to early autumn, are to 2in. (5cm.) across. Viticella Group. (3)

'Royal Velvet' Velvety purple flowers typify this free-flowering, early large-flowering cultivar. It is ideal for containers or for use in small gardens. (1)

'Royalty' A.G.M. Semi-double mauve flowers appear in late spring and early summer, rich purple-colored single flowers in early autumn. This is a good subject for a container. Lanuginosa and Patens Groups. (2)

'Ruby Glow' A Jim Fisk introduction from 1975, this compact plant has rosy mauve sepals and flowers from early summer to early autumn. It does well in containers or small gardens. Lanuginosa Group. (1)

'Scartho Gem' Introduced by Pennells in 1973, this early large-flowered cultivar has bright pink sepals with wavy edges that are slightly overlapping. Patens Group. (1)

'Sealand Gem' A seedling of 'Bees' Jubilee', this early large-flowered clematis, with flowers up to 4³⁄₄in. (12cm.) across, is free-flowering and continues into early autumn. Lanuginosa Group. (2)

'Serenata' The sepals of this 1960 cultivar are dark purple with a reddish-purple bar, contrasting well with its yellow stamens. Flowering from late spring to early autumn, it grows up to 10ft. (3m.). Jackmanii Group. (2)

serratifolia This true species from Korea and China is named after the serrated edges of the leaves. The flowers, which appear from mid-summer to mid-autumn, are like those of orientalis but with pale yellow sepals and dark filaments. It has a floppy nature and can be used for ground cover. (3)

'Silver Moon' A.G.M. This early large-flowered clematis

C. 'Victoria'

has silver-mauve flowers up to 6in. (15cm.) from spring to autumn and is good in containers. Lanuginosa Group. (2)

'Sir Trevor Lawrence' The Jackmans first raised this cultivar in 1890 from a cross of *C. texensis* and 'Star of India' A.G.M. The flowers, seen in summer and early autumn, are purple-red with a scarlet band along the center. Texensis Group. (3)

'Snow Queen' This has both early and late crops of flowers that are essentially white with suffusions of palest pink or blue. (1)

'Södertälje' Pink-red sepals up to 3³⁄₄ in. (8cm.) across typify this cultivar raised in Sweden in 1952. It grows well in trees and flowers from mid-summer to autumn. Viticella Group. (3)

songarica Native to Asia, this herbaceous plant grows to 5ft. (1.5m.) Its summer to early autumn flowers are small but intricately pretty, with white, reflexed sepals, citrus-green filaments and maroon anthers. (3)

'Souvenir du Capitaine Thuilleaux' Strawberries and cream sum up this large hybrid, since the sepals are cream with a strawberry bar. It grows to 13ft. (4m.) and flowers from early summer to early autumn. Patens Group. (1)

stans Native to Japan, this species has white or bluish, tubular flowers and reflexed sepals. The plant grows to 3ft. (1m.) and flowers from mid-summer to autumn. (3)

'Star of India' A.G.M. Introduced in 1867 by Girault in France, this red-maroon cultivar flowers from mid- to late summer. Patens and Jackmanii Groups. (3)

'Sugar Candy' ('Evione') A striking cultivar introduced by Evison/Poulsen in 1994, this has pink-mauve flowers with a darker bar, which are up to 7in. (18cm.) across. It flowers from mid-summer to mid-autumn and does best in the sun. Patens Group. (1)

'Sylvia Denny' Pure white, semi-double flowers, up to 4in. (10cm.) across, are produced in spring, summer and early autumn on a compact plant. (1)

tangutica This is a native species of China and Mongolia with vigorous growth up to about 13ft. (4m.) and small, yellow, cup-shaped flowers. It occurs in a variety of forms. (2)

terniflora A species clematis native to Japan, this vigorous vine can cover up to 20ft. (6m.). It flowers in autumn, thus its other name of 'Sweet fall scented clematis'. (3)

'The Bride' The flower is of a typical jackmanii form, with a pure white color tinged with the faintest greenish yellow and soft yellow stamens. It flowers in early summer. Jackmanii Group. (2)

'The President' A.G.M. A classic raised by Charles Noble in 1876, the flowers are large, up to 6in. (15cm.) across, with bright purple flowers and red anthers. It flowers for a long period in summer and, being compact, is ideal for containers or small gardens. Patens Group. (1)

x *triternata* 'Rubromarginata' A.G.M. Growing vigorously to smother a wall in its red-edged flowers, this is an excellent, summer clematis. It is highly scented. (3)

'Twilight' Easy to grow, this cultivar has uniform, pale pink sepals on top with a broad, greenish bar on the underside. A late spring and mid-summer flowerer, it does well in containers. Jackmanii Group. (2)

'Vanessa' Lavender-pink flowers with yellow stamens are typical of this hybrid raised by Vince and Sylvia Denny in 1995 from 'Sylvia Denny' and 'Perle d'Azur A.G.M. It grows well over a wall or pergola. Jackmanii Group. (2)

x *vedrariensis* A hybrid between *C. chrysocoma* and *C. montana*, this produces flowers about 2in. (5cm.) across, which range from mauve to pink to rose, in spring. (1)

'Venosa Violacea' A.G.M. One of the finest clematis known, this has a color scheme of white and purple. It grows well in a container or up a wall and flowers from mid-summer to early autumn. Viticella Group. (3)

'Veronica's Choice' Raised by the Pennells, the pale lavender, fragrant flowers are double in early summer and single later on. Lanuginosa Group. (1)

'Victoria' Distinctive, mauve-pink flowers are up to 5¹⁄₂ in. (14cm.) across and are produced from mid- to late summer. It was raised by Cripps & Sons in 1867. Jackmanii Group. (3)

'Ville de Lyon' A reliable cultivar, the flowers have burnished red sepals and a yellow-orange boss. It flowers from early to late summer and is best displayed among roses or buddleia that can support it. Viticella Group. (3)

'Vino' ('Poulvo') Raised by Evison/Poulsen in Denmark, this has petunia-red flowers and yellow anthers. Its flowers are up to 4³⁄₄ in. (12cm.) across and borne from late spring to the end of summer. Jackmanii Group. (1)

'Violet Charm' Named after its violet-blue flowers, this was raised in Birmingham, England in 1966. It flowers from early to late summer and is ideal for cut flowers or for use in a container. Lanuginosa Group. (2)

viorna A species clematis native from Georgia to Texas in the United States, this is also known as the leather flower or vase vine. Its small bell-like flowers are soft pink with reflexed sepals. (3)

vitalba This is a true species clematis, native to southern Europe and north Africa. It flowers from mid-summer to well into the autumn. Its small clusters of creamy white flowers are slightly scented. The plant is very vigorous. (2)

viticella This species clematis is native to southern Europe through to west Asia. It is vigorous, growing to 13ft. (4m.) and its bell-shaped flowers are blue, purple or rose-purple in mid-summer. (3)

viticella 'Purpurea Plena Elegans' A.G.M. One of the prettiest of the smallest, double flowers, this cultivar grows 10–13ft. (3–4m.). The red-maroon flowers are produced in large quantities in summer to early autumn. Viticella Group. (3)

'Vyvyan Pennell' A.G.M. Purple, mauve and blue double or semi-double flowers are produced in early summer, followed by single flowers in late summer. The plant is susceptible to wilt. Florida and Patens Groups. (2)

'Wada's Primrose' From Japan in the 1970s, this pale yellow clematis has faintly scented flowers up to 6in. (15cm.) across and does well in containers in full sun. Patens Group. It flowers in spring, summer and early autumn. (1)

'W.E. Gladstone' One of the larger summer to autumn-flowering clematis, this was raised in England in 1881. It has blue-purple sepals up to 8in. (20cm.) long and red stamens. Lanuginosa Group. (2)

'Will Goodwin' A.G.M. Flowering from early to late summer, this cultivar, introduced in England in 1961, has mid-blue sepals and bright yellow anthers. Its flowers are up to 6in. (15cm.). Lanuginosa Group. (2)

'William Kennett' An older clematis, raised in England in 1875, this has lilac-blue sepals and dark red anthers and flowers from summer to autumn. Lanuginosa Group. (2)

Clematis structure

CLEMATIS 'FLOWERS' are not strictly flowers as they are known in the botanical world but are made up of the brightly colored parts of the sepals. In normal flowers, the sepals are green and unobtrusive, lying underneath the colored petals. However, in clematis the petals are absent and the color is provided instead by the sepals.

The edge, or margin, of the sepals is often described as crimped or crenulated to illustrate its relative wavyness. There are often other diagnostic colors running down the midline of the sepals which are often of a darker hue than the rest of the sepal, and this feature is called the bar.

The female reproductive parts of the clematis consist of three elements, as in other plants: the stigma, style and ovary. The female parts are less obvious than the male parts but the stigma is the receptive area which becomes dusted with pollen, while the style is the neck or passageway to the ovary. The ovary contains the seed. After fertilisation, the ovary swells up and becomes obvious. Each developing seed is surmounted by a long, fluffy tail that allows it to be dispersed in the wind. The male parts, or stamens, comprise two separate elements: the filament and the anthers. The filament carries the anthers, which contain the male reproductive cells, or pollen. The color of the anthers and filaments are diagnostic features for individual identification of clematis. Collectively, the male and female parts are called the boss.

Clematis leaves are also interesting since many of them are trifoliate, meaning that the leaf is made of three leaflets. The leaves are paired on the stem, typical of members of the buttercup family. The whole leaf is therefore made up of the three leaflets and a stalk, or petiole, which may be twisted to aid climbing. If the margin of the leaflets is toothed, this is referred to as serrated. The distance between the leaves is known as the internode, and the node is where the pair of leaves arises on the stem.

PLANT HARDINESS ZONES

In America, the USDA hardiness zone system is based on the average annual minimum temperature for each zone. Most of the plants in the Clematis A-Z on pages 110-121 are deemed to be hardy–that is, they will survive in the coldest zonal ranges, from zones 1–6. All those plants that will not survive in these temperatures are denoted with a * symbol to show that they are tender and should be grown in zone 7 and above.

	Fahrenheit	Celsius
Zone 1	below -50º	below -46º
Zone 2	-50º to -40º	-46º to -40º
Zone 3	-40º to -30º	-40º to -34º
Zone 4	-30º to -20º	-34º to -29º
Zone 5	-20º to -10º	-29º to -23º
Zone 6	-10º to 0º	-23º to -18º
Zone 7	0º to 10º	-18º to -12º
Zone 8	10º to 20º	-12º to -7º
Zone 9	20º to 30º	-7º to -1º
Zone 10	30º to 40º	-1º to 4º
Zone 11	above 40º	above 4º

Buying clematis

Clematis are fast becoming mass-produced for the retail market, resulting in millions of plants moving each year within Europe and from Europe to North America to meet the demand. There are two recommended places to buy clematis: at your local garden center or from a specialist grower.

At most garden centers, the choice of species and cultivars is generally limited to popular varieties. For a greater range, it is best to find a specialist grower in your own country. Seed merchants also stock a limited range of clematis species and cultivars for worldwide distribution by mail-order.

Purchase and exchange of seeds is also possible between members of national clematis societies and the International Clematis Society (Secretary: Fiona Woolfenden, 3 Cuthberts Close, Waltham Cross, EN7 5RB, England. email: clematis@dial.pipex.com Web site: http://dialspace.dial.pipex.com/clematis/) Southern California Clematis Society: P.O. Box 17085, Irvine, CA 92623-7085. Web site: http/members.aol.com/clematissc/

Notes on photography

NINETY-FIVE PER cent of the images in this book were taken with a Bronica ETRSi, with a standard Zenza Bronica lens, which has an Ultra-Violet (UVO) filter permanently screwed on. For closer work, this was supported by an E-14 extension tube, and for extremely close work by a screw-on x2 close-up lens. I determined the f stop of all images, leaving the Bronica to automate the exposure. With optimum lens efficiency at about f.8–11 (producing the best results), this f stop was often sought, yet on very sunny days many images were taken at f.22—the maximum for this lens. Tripod work was essential for successful results. Although I refer to shoot in sunshine, there are many images in this book photographed in shade, either because of necessity or because the nearby light was overly bright. Often more depth of color is apparent in full shade than in full sun.

I am not a great fan of 35mm images yet with the tiny, bell-like clematis I had no option but to use my Canon—and even flash. In tests, many 35mm flash shots actually turned out sharper than Bronica close-ups, although not reliably. Many of the small viticellas are expert at making themselves unphotogenic, hanging their bells this way and that, often half way up a tree. Most of the clematis photographed in this book were therefore shot in natural daylight and their colors are generally true. The film used throughout has been Fujichrome 100 ASA, which I find reproduces colors impeccably. It is within the realms of blues and purples that the faithful reproduction of real color is somewhat lost. Although this does not happen with every clematis belonging to this color group, it seems that some plants either reflect or absorb different quantities of ultra-violet light from the sun, causing a divergent color effect on the film. Most of the images in this book were taken outside, so the clematis look as bright and perky as they would in the garden. Only a few were shot under tents, in which case a flash was used to avoid an orange glow, which often results from taking photos under cover. For inspiration, I have visited many wonderful gardens in the U.K., such as Kew, Wisley, Sissinghurst and Christopher Lloyd's Great Dixter, as well as the Montpelier Botanic Gardens in Languedoc, France, the Bagatelle Gardens in Paris, France and gardens near Wurzburg, Germany.

My quest for native clematis has taken me to the wilder parts of the French and Austrian Alps, to the dry foothills of California and the humid north-east coast of the U.S.A. I have also searched for and photographed clematis in the Czech Republic and Slovakia while writing this book.

Nomenclature

THE WORLD OF clematis is fraught with name changes, synonymy and plain confusion, with various individuals offering up different names for the same selections, sometimes a century after they have been given their original names. The original names of all plants—and animals for that matter—are always the correct ones. With the introduction of trade names, the same clematis may also exist under a different hybrid name. Generally, clematis are known either by their specific name, which is their latin name, or by their hybrid or clone name. Most clematis do not have English common names and many of the central European plants have their own common names, which are not English.

The genus name of Clematis refers to all clematis and it is in the buttercup (*Ranunculaceae*) family. In this book, true species clematis are listed accorded to their correct specific name. A characteristic of a species is that it will always breeds true, that is produce seedlings looking like itself. Hybrids are listed with their names following the Clematis genus name, as in *C.* 'Vino', or to show to which plants they are closely related, as in *C. alpina* 'Ruby', which may at times be shortened to *C.a.* 'Ruby'. If a cross is made between two species, these hybrids are referred to with an "x", as in *C.* x *eriostemon*. If, within a selection of individuals, some are different from normal then a clone is produced. This is illustrated in the case of *C.* x *cartmanii* 'Joe', for example—'Joe' being the clone.

The letters A.G.M. after a plant name refer to the Award of Garden Merit, denoting those plants which the British Royal Horticultural Society recognises as being of outstanding excellence for garden decoration or use.

Index

Acknowledgments

I would like to thank a lot of people who have been instrumental in putting this work together, not least Susan Berry, Ginny Surtees, Mandy Lebentz and Helen Collins. Thanks also to Claudine Meissner, who helped with some of the design. I am delighted that Mary Toomey, editor of *The Clematis*, the official publication of the Clematis Society, was able to provide a foreword. I would also like to extend my thanks to the members of the Clematis Society and of the International Clematis Society, who welcomed me to their gardens,many of whom are mentioned below.

This book has been a long time germinating but it has seen me traveling throughout Europe and North America in a quest for special shots of clematis, often accompanied by my wife, Carol, who has engaged my enthusiasm for the genus. Sarah Caffyn, my assistant, with her keen eye for a brilliant image, has objectively sought the best for this book. To them, many thanks.

The clematis in this book have been photographed in numerous gardens and I would like to extend my special thanks to Sally Gadd, formerly of Sussex Clematis Nursery, England, for taking me through so many old varieties; Malcolm Oviatt-Ham at his nursery in Willingham, Cambridgeshire; Sheila Chapman at her nursery in Chelmsford, Essex; Tony Hutchins at his County Park Nursery in Essex; and Harry Caddick at Caddick's Clematis Nursery in Warrington, Cheshire, England. My thanks also to Brother Stefan Franczak at his monastic clematis garden in Warsaw, Poland; and to Mr and Mrs Ed Sampson of Mourning Cloak Botanic Garden, Tehachapi, California.

Of the many private gardens I have visited in the U.K., I am very grateful to the following: Kath, Alan and Nick Goode for allowing me unfettered access to their wonderful garden in East Sussex; Vera and Tony Orsbourne in Sellinge, Kent; Joy Anderson near Ashdown Forest in East Sussex; Ben Clifton near Paddock Wood, Kent; Everett and Carol Leeds in Betchworth, Surrey; Mike and Mary Brown at Clematis Corner, Shillingford, Oxon; Brian and Joyce Hargreaves in Rye, East Sussex; Mick and Mary Dean in Marlow, Bucks; Mr. and Mrs. O'Brien in Hoo, East Sussex; Mr and Mrs Geoff Leece in Catsfield, East Sussex and Miriam Rothschild at Ashton, Northants.